Pen to Paper
A Beginner's Guide

Vera Cáit Walsh

Boland Press

First published 2020
Text copyright © Vera Walsh

Boland Press
Grove Mill
Hollyfort
Co. Wexford

http://bolandpress.blogspot.com

A CIP catalogue record for this book
is available from the British Library
ISBN: 978-1-907855 -27-6

www.facebook.com/vera.walsh.5872
http://veracait.blogspot.com

Cover image@maudis60/123RF.com

Cover design by Boland Press

Author photograph by Ken Kelly

Printed in Ireland by
Sprintprint

HELLO

My name is Vera Cáit Walsh and I'd like to share with you my personal take on Creative Writing.

For me, Creative Writing is a form of therapy. When I put pen to paper I am transported into the 'inner' me, where I begin to realise how much I love to write, and become aware of hidden treasures that I have almost forgotten. I become aware of myself as an artist.

The written word guides me along the way I want to go, to delve into my spiritual self, and become aware of all the beautiful people and places that I hold in my heart. I am also transported into a world of make-believe, using my imagination to step into another life, another me.

The gift of being a writer is a treasure to be valued and used, always. I hope you, the reader, will be inspired by *Pen to Paper* and my writings, and discover for yourself the gift and joy of Creative Writing.

I dedicate this book to all the people who have encouraged me to follow my interest in writing.

A very special 'Thank You' to my brother Liam who has supported and encouraged me to follow my desire to become a good writer.

The SOL Community and its founder, Kevin, have always been a wonderful support and encouragement. Without their help, my book *Pen to Paper* would still be a dream.

To all my writing friends, thank you.

Contents

PART 1

PART 2

PART 3

PART 4

PART 5

Stories and Plays

by Vera Cáit Walsh

Pen to Paper

PART 1

Therapy in Writing

This book is about Creative Writing and the benefits of putting words on paper. There is a therapy to be found in Creative Writing, it allows us to express our thoughts in word-form, revealing the 'inner child', even to ourselves. This is a great help in dealing with the stresses of life, where hidden thoughts and secrets of the mind may be revealed by writing about how we feel, and how to look at life in different ways.

Writing down our anxieties and fears is a good way to deal with feelings of low self-esteem or depression.

Creative Writing can prove to be an aid in stepping away from our normal thinking patterns, allowing us to explore this wonderful world of ours, creatively.

This book contains guided prompts and exercises in Creative Writing with examples of poetry, plays, stories and memoirs written by me.

Enjoy the creative journey!

One of the mysteries of the human mind is that we do not know ourselves well enough, or we have an image of ourselves that is incorrect.

1

A lot of what we think and do are responses to programmes that we have learned as a child, perhaps instilled into us by our parents or mentors. There is a good reason for all the quirks and ways we have of doing things, yet our reasoning may not be justified. It is so important to get to the root cause of who we are and why we are inclined to do certain things. Self-knowledge is the road to health of mind, body and spirit.

Writing creatively is a good aid in getting to know ourselves. As we open our minds and hearts to the words we write, we learn to reveal who we are to ourselves and to others.

How much you want to do this is up to you. Yet, as soon as we apply pen to paper, we set ourselves on the road to discovering our true selves.

It began with an accident

My therapy in writing began with an accident. We lived in the west of Ireland, and I foolishly went out on my moped without considering the fierce Atlantic wind.

After a spell in hospital, I found myself at home in bed, with time on my hands. My interest in creative writing came to my rescue, and I began to write plays and short stories, and even a TV script.

There was no end to my enthusiasm, and my friends humoured me by acting out my TV script. I have to agree, it would not have won any prizes, yet I was amazed and encouraged. I put words on paper, and they came alive in the characters my friends played out. So, this is what Creative Writing is all about.

Later, I had the chance to do a course with the Irish Writers Centre, 'Writing for the Media', and before long I knew I had found my 'writing voice'.

Whenever time allowed, I continued to write. This time, more modestly, writing short stories and plays. Happily, it turned out that my forte and success lies in playwriting.

Anyone Can Write

For the person who would like to write, yet feels they cannot, the answer is simple: *pen to paper.*

If one can read and write, then the potential is there to become a good writer. Most professional writers will tell us, all that is needed is

10% inspiration and 90% work.

The 10% inspiration comes from being true to oneself and having the courage to write about it.

I was at a poetry reading once where I was impressed by the honesty of the poet. His poems were based in 50s Dublin, which was interesting enough. Yet, it was the story of his life and of his adoption, and years later discovering that his favourite aunt was in fact his birth mother, that inspired me.

3

The audience were captivated by his openness and courage. Emotionally, it cost him, yet he gained his freedom by sharing his truth. This is a way to self-knowledge.

Not all of us may want to open our hearts to the world, yet in our endeavours to put thoughts on paper there is a natural therapy taking place. So, let us begin putting PEN TO PAPER.

Craft of Writing Creatively

Regard writing as a CRAFT. For example, woodwork is a craft, knitting is a craft, yet without the basic learning techniques one would never be able to knit or use tools for woodwork.

How can one develop the craft of Creative Writing? Begin by learning the basics.

A writer writes:

GIVE TIME to writing

WRITE about what you know

READ a lot

Use your IMAGINATION

Use your EMOTIONS

ENJOY the creative journey

Simply WRITE.

Creative Writing Techniques

Much is said about being creative, especially with words. In Ireland, we are blessed with great writers of literature displayed in works of fiction, poetry and memoirs.

We are a nation of storytellers, and this is often found in our Irish language where the very words used come from the heart, i.e. Ta bron orm (there is sorrow on me), and Grá mo croí (love of my heart).

Most of us are comfortable with writing in English, and some are experts with the spoken word, becoming a wordsmith with an ability to put vision into the written word.

For myself, I love writing and being creative in using my imagination to create characters and stories.

My favourite way of writing is as a playwright. As soon as I put pen to paper the imagined characters come to life. They almost speak for themselves, using words that denote their personality. A lady will always speak like a lady, paying great respect to the English language. A country lass will speak plainly, giving colour to the choice of words she uses, i.e. *'and what would you be wanting to do the likes of that for?'*

It can be fun, creating a character who is different to ourselves, and yet we will understand them so well, because in each one of us there is a world of personalities.

Just like a baby learns to walk and talk by example, so we too learn to understand and take on board the lives and ways of other people.

 Creative Writing is fun

 Take pen to paper and write

 Be surprised and delighted with results

When it comes to Creative Writing, it is important to be passionate about writing. We may lack the correct words to express how we feel, or even the right spelling, yet if we write with passion then the words will lift off the page.

It is almost miraculous how certain thoughts and ideas come to mind and, if we have the courage to put them into our writings, we will surprise ourselves and please our reader.

Originality is the key to good writing and can lead to great writing. However, it is important not to want to impress either the reader or ourselves by using words that sound 'posh'. Posh words are usually artificial and can lead us to act and pretend, instead of being real.

When we put words on paper and are pleased with the result, then we are on the road to becoming a truly good writer, perhaps even a great one.

Technical Side of Writing

The desire to write creatively comes alive when we put pen to paper, or fingers on keyboard. As with every craft, tools are needed, and a very practical side to writing is making a list. I would put on that list:

> A QUIET PLACE to write
> COMPUTER
> DICTIONARY

THESAURUS
BOOKS relating to writing
CLASSICS
BOOKS by authors that one enjoys reading
A TIMER
Suitable TIME for writing
NATURE WALK

Walking in nature is one of the most encouraging ways of opening our minds and imagination to the wonderful craft of Creative Writing.

Become a regular visitor to the local library and, if possible, join a Creative Writing Group. We can be shy about sharing our writing pieces with others, yet I would say, face whatever fears you might have. Deliberately put yourself forward and delve into different ways of expressing yourself as a writer.

Share your writing with encouraging friends.

Read in public if the opportunity arises. This can be a formidable challenge and extremely rewarding when faced.

First and foremost, believe that you can write.

Here is a short story I wrote some time ago:

Soul Mate

She closed the book, slowly.

He waited, tapping his foot. 'Well?'

Eleanor looked into his earnest face. She believed in truth. In being direct, no hedging or fuss. Take it or leave it. Yet, for once she found herself unable to speak out her inner thoughts, her convictions.

He depended on her opinion. She knew what this book meant to him; what it had cost him to lay bare his soul on every page. The writing was good, above average at best, and the subject matter? Oh, everything in her wanted to scream out, 'Rubbish'.

'Well?' He trusted her. He would be guided by her opinion.

Eleanor smiled. 'The best yet.'

His face lit up with sheer relief and, springing to his feet, he hugged her. 'I had to say it, the way it is. Oh, I'm glad you understand.'

But Eleanor did not understand. It broke her heart to know the truth at last. All these years she had believed she was the love of his life. The bond between them was so strong.

It was only now, having read his book which gave such a descriptive outline of his love for another; every touch and kiss and embrace; the union of his soul with someone he loved deeply, that Eleanor realised how their lives had grown apart. He had found his soulmate.

Does every mother suffer this pain of losing their only son's undivided love?

It was time to let him go.

Short Story Guideline

Here are some easy guidelines to writing a short story:

Passion
Whatever we have a passion for, write about it. Ensure we have a good knowledge of the subject.

Character
Make our characters 'real'. Let them come to life.

Focus
Check that the story is leading somewhere and has a goal. Your story needs to develop.

First Draft
Just write ALL down. Keep writing even if it seems to make no sense. Keep the 'inner critic' quiet.

Research
Make sure all the FACTS are correct. Give a realistic history to the characters.

Re-Draft
Produce a flowing, coherent story. Let each word earn its keep.

Final Draft
Revise the story. Release the critic. When happy with the result, find a publisher.

Here is another short story from my pen:

Even Cows Pray

Fr Grey was having a bad day, again. His frustration could hardly be contained. After all, wasn't the Parish Committee supposed to help and relieve him of some surplus duties. Instead he felt lumbered with personalities that would drive a saint to drink, and he was not a saint by any means.

If they could only agree among themselves and cut out all the pontificating and bickering and get on with getting things done.

'God help us,' he muttered as he left the community centre, got into his relic of a car, and drove up to the church.

It was dark when he got there, yet there were movements in the graveyard. As his eyes became accustomed to the dark, he could see -

'Oh, Lord,' Danny Fay's sheep were all over the graveyard, eating the grass, and the flowers off the graves.

'Whoosh, whoosh, get out of here. Go!'

With the help of a stick, he chased them out the gate and closed it tight. The rain began to pour down, causing a rivulet of muddy water. Not a good time for Fr Grey to realise his lovely polished shoes leaked!

'I'm definitely going to ring the Bishop about the Curate he promised me. I'm too old for all this . . . this stuff. Forty years and nothing to show for it. Oh, God help me.' He went off muttering to himself, as he got into his car. He removed his soaked jacket and drove home.

Mary, the part-time housekeeper, was in a huff.

'Spend me time cooking a decent meal. Sure, all the good's gone out of it now.' She slapped the bowl onto the table. Then, with her nose in the air, she put on her coat and went off about her business.

Fr Grey looked at the bowl of half-burnt stew; sprinkled it with salt and got it down as best he could. Afterwards, he sat into the armchair by the ebbing fire, book in hand and, within minutes, fell fast asleep.

The cock crowing in a neighbour's field startled him back to life.

'Bless us and save us, almost 7 o'clock in the morning! Ah, what a great sleep.'

He stretched his stiff body and gave himself a quick wash, remembering the personal comments made by a certain lady when she was in the confession box. He was sorely tempted to have her say a Rosary for her penance.

'Ah, perhaps it's no harm to get a bit of criticism now and then, whether we like it or not.' Fr Grey was feeling a lot better today and determined to go easy in judging the faults of others. A nice hot cup of tea and bit of toast and he was ready to face the world, or so he thought.

When he got to the church, he noticed a good crowd had gathered. Suddenly, he realised he was still wearing his slippers! Was that why everybody seemed to be staring at him? There was something else. Oh, Lord, he had forgotten to close up the church last night. Had something terrible happened?

He rushed forward, but Danny Fay stopped him. 'Father, sorry about the sheep, and . . . '

'Yes, yes, the church?'

Members of the parish committee came rushing up to him.

'Oh, Father, it's terrible, so it is.'

'Yes, terrible,' echoed someone. They all followed him as he hurried into the church.

Fr Grey stood speechless as he looked up at the altar. There was someone there bent over. Praying? As he got closer, he recognised the body. No. It couldn't be! He stepped back in disbelief and felt his slippers slide into a sticky, smelly mess.

'Oh, shit.' Danny Fay's milking cow had done its business all over the aisle.

A silent crowd watched as Fr Grey fell down on his knees, his shoulders shaking with emotion. Next moment he was almost choking as he attempted to hold back the laughter. Tears rolled down his face, as he laughed and laughed. The whole congregation joined in, filling the rafters with the strangest sound of music never heard before.

Fr Grey smiled, 'Can life get better than this?'

Creative Writing Workshop

Sometimes we need a little help to get the writing juices flowing. Using a KEY to open up the imagination can help. In this example, we can use the mnemonic ABLE:

A ART OF WRITING:
Regard writing as an ART form.

B BUILD:
Build on ideas and thoughts that arise.

L LOVE the written word:
Have a 'love affair' with matching words.

E EDIT / EDUCATE:
Be brave when editing what you have written. Study formats and authenticity of the written word.

Prompts

Visual Images
Another way to prod the imagination is with visual images. You can use pictures from a book or magazine or take a trip to an art gallery.

A Given Time

Write a piece about yourself starting, 'When I was 10 / 20 / 30 / 40 years old.' Our imagination can take us to any age.

Emotions

Creative writing comes into its own when we are moved by our emotions. Just calling to mind an experience of gladness, sadness, even madness will get the writing flowing.

Write about an emotional experience such as

    BIRTHDAY
    WEDDING
    FUNERAL
    SUCCESS

and be as objective as you possible can.

PART 2

Creating History

To write creatively, we need to give the characters we create a background, a history of their lives.

Ask questions such as:

Where do they come from?
City or country?
Are they educated?
Are they 'of the earth'?
Parents, siblings, relations?
Close friends / casual friends?
Married or single?
What kind of past do they have?
Is there a secret that cannot be told?
What kind of personality do they have?
Are they happy?

The more creative we are in building up our characters, the more 'fodder' for writing. Let the imagination go wild. Also, good to remember that you yourself have a history, and this will help you in writing your memoirs.

The following is a story outlining the development of characterisation.

The Painting

Marie was surprised at how calm she felt. If all had gone as planned, she would be married now. She began to realise that she had not been ready. Perhaps she would never be ready. Who's to say. At any rate, it hadn't happened, and apart from the shock and expense of the hotel, and all the disappointed guests and, of course, her poor Aunt Nora. 'Oh, what would your mother say, God rest her soul, if she was here today. Oh, we'll never live this down, never, never.'

Marie listened without listening.

The scribbled note Shane, the best man, had handed her, lay crumpled up in her lap.

'Jimmy asked me to give this to you. Marie, I'm so sorry.'

It was the kind way he said it that caused her to cry. The compassion in his voice touched her, and so the tears flowed, while Aunt Nora practically damned Jimmy for his cowardly act. Yet, was it cowardly?

Now, two months later, Marie felt more aware of what had come between her and Jimmy . . . the painting.

It had been a lovely, summer Sunday. Then the heavens opened, and she and Jimmy had to rush for cover. The National Art Gallery was nearby, so in they went.

Marie slipped into the Ladies, sticking her wet hair under the dryer, and letting the hot air blow freely down her wet blouse. Presentable, she came out looking for Jimmy. There he was, looking transfixed. He was staring at the figure of a beautiful young lady, dressed in an almost transparent, white Brittany wedding dress. The lady in question was the focal point of a famous painting, *The Convent Garden,* by John William Leech.

Jimmy's attraction to the painting was easy to understand. A sensitive and beautifully crafted piece of work. The lady in white, the painter's wife, displayed an innocence one would expect to find in a young novice, deep in prayer. The rest of the figures in the background were reputed to be nuns, hence the title *The Convent Garden.* The foreground was filled with long-stemmed flowers, irises and roses, swaying in the imagined breeze that blew through the garden.

Marie loved the painting. She occupied herself with reading about John William Leech. She commented to Jimmy that the artist was born in Dublin in 1881 and died in Surrey in 1968, only to realise his attention was riveted on the lady in white. He was oblivious to all, including Marie.

That is when the awful pangs of jealousy set in. Marie told herself how foolish this was, and yet the circumstances that followed this first encounter with the painting, reaffirmed and heightened Marie's jealousy.

Every Sunday, rain or shine, Jimmy felt compelled to visit the Art Gallery. He would go directly to the painting and stand, blatantly admiring his new-found love. Marie was both furious and curious. Could a painting really have such an effect on a person? Granted, the young lady was beautiful, Marie could not deny that. Yet, maybe this was just a ploy on Jimmy's part to let her know she was no longer the love of his life, as he used to say so many times when they were first courting.

She sought advice from her good friend, Shane, best man to be. He made light of it. 'Jimmy's like that. Gets fixed on something and feels a compulsion to follow it to the death. Don't worry about it.'

Marie felt relieved. But what else could it be? She knew Jimmy had loved her once. Somehow, this strange love for a figure in a painting seemed to blot out his love for her. It wasn't that he loved her less, no, he just loved the lady in white more.

Marie now realised how unwise she had been. If she had simply walked away, or returned his engagement ring, then perhaps he would have realised what was happening. But, no, Marie had fought to keep his love, remonstrating with him for daydreaming and not paying attention to her. Very, very wrong. This just pushed him away and deeper into his inner world of fantasy.

Marie stopped going to the Art Gallery with Jimmy. He wanted to. She did not. It was as simple as that. Pity that the wedding plans had already gone under way. It isn't easy to take time-out and re-assess a situation when it's already been planned a year in advance. Getting married to Jimmy was all Marie ever wanted, or so she thought. He would be the father of her children and they would be friends for life. Boy, how wrong she had been.

She realised now that Jimmy had been too accommodating. He was happy to let her plan the wedding. It was she who decided when they would marry and where they would go on their honeymoon, and even where they would live. Marie had known about the town houses being built near where she worked, and that special-savings bonus had come just on time for putting down a deposit.

It had all been too easy. They never rowed. Whenever they had a difference of opinion, Jimmy simply gave in and agreed to do whatever she wanted. That was suspect.

Shane had told her about the relationship Jimmy had with his former girlfriend, and how they fought about everything, and how terrible it had been for Jimmy. Took him ages to get over it, he said.

Did he get over it? A man needs spunk! The Jimmy that Marie had fallen in love with was all love, but no spunk. So, what kind of love was that?

If it hadn't been for Shane, Marie just did not know what she would have done. Her head told her it was all for the best, yet her emotions were not that reasonable. Tears came too easily. A word said with the slightest off-tone and she was devastated.

Marie had good friends and they cared, yet it was hard for them to disguise their pity. 'Poor Marie. Left at the altar. So sad.' What she didn't overhear, she read in the sympathetic glances they gave her. Shane was the only one who offered her good company, without pity. Marie found herself laughing, even being able to make fun of herself and her misguided past. They became good friends, and more.

'Hello, Marie,' Jimmy walked towards her. It was inevitable they would meet again, living in the same town. Marie was unprepared for the encounter.

Jimmy extended his hand. Mechanically, Marie extended hers. The touch sent a tremor through her nervous system and she worked hard to control her emotions. Pleasantries and apologies were passed. Jimmy was truly sorry for letting her down. Those were not the words Marie wanted to hear. The ultimate shock was yet to come. An elegant young lady dressed in white approached them. Marie stared. It was as if the lady in the painting had come to life.

'Marie, this is Angelina. We . . .'

Angelina stepped forward. 'Marie, so nice to meet you. Jimmy and I are old, **old** friends.'

Images – A Means to Write

Visual images, i.e. pictures and objects, can be used to stimulate our creative imagination. This allows us to focus on the visual and write about whatever comes to mind.

Creative writing is an art-form to be used wisely. In a way, writers become the characters they write about. This gives a sense of reality to each character; they become 'real' people, making 'real' choices, living 'real' lives.

When we learn to use our imagination as a **tool,** then we may even surprise ourselves at the lives we write about.

More Prompts:

Become an **OBJECT**
An umbrella / paint brush / pencil
table / chair / computer / hat

Become an **ANIMAL**
Horse / donkey / dog / cat / mouse /
fish / frog / bird /tiger

Become of the **EARTH**
Flower / tree / field / potato / carrot /
cabbage / turnip / straw

The following is a short example of writing as an object.

My Family Tree

I grew up on farmer Brown's place with my parents and siblings. It was a strange place at first and very cold, especially when the snow came. My parents were afraid that I wouldn't survive, yet I did.

When spring came, I was delighted to see all the green fields and especially the beautiful yellow daffodils and the birds twittering around chasing butterflies.

Farmer Brown is a kind man and cares about the earth and all that grows on it, so we are well looked after. However, when winter came again the troubles started. Heavy rain flooded many of the lovely green fields and the wind. Oh, the stormy wind was the worst of all. I didn't fully understand what was happening, yet the pain and worry on my mother's face told me that terrible things were going to happen.

My father was the first to go. He tried so desperately to hold out, to fight the awful storm, but it was no use. He collapsed with a fierce thud and never recovered.

My mother was next to go, and nobody could save her. Perhaps she also wanted to be with my father. My siblings and I were broken hearted, yet we survived.

Farmer Brown did the best he could, and I knew he would look after what was left of us.

Another summer has come, and I'm more grown up and able to stretch out and let the world see just how beautiful I am. A poet came by the other day and sat down beside me. He began to write down words and quietly sing them out loud. 'I wish that I could ever see, a poem as lovely as a tree.'

He would have loved my parents.

Appetite

The dictionary describes APPETITE as an enthusiasm for something.

Whatever we are enthusiastic about **will** happen. Your interest alone will push you forward and supply you with energy to fulfil your desires. This is especially important when it comes to creative writing. Thoughts and ideas buzz around in our head, compelling us to write, and so we will.

Human nature, or just being tired or troubled, can cause us to lose our enthusiasm for writing. The secret is to allow personal space (meditation helps) and, whatever method you use, make sure it works.

We are such unique creatures in every way that personal quiet and special time is needed. Imagine yourself as a creative child who is hungry to write.

This appetite will gnaw at you. It is so precious that it cannot be denied, unless, that is, we deny ourselves the opportunity to sit down and write.

Ability to Focus

When it comes to Creative Writing, it is so easy to lose focus. We start off with a wonderful idea and, before we have put pen to paper, we can so easily lose focus. Perhaps this is caused by a lack of preparation.

The first step in creative writing is learning to put our ideas on paper in a structured way. For example, one wants to write a short story and the idea for the story has already crept into our mind. Now for the exciting part, putting our idea into words. This can be simple when we are in the flow, so to say. However, it will require you to focus and ask questions:

Who / Why / What / When

Who am I writing about
Why am I writing this
What am I writing about
When will all this happen

Easy to see there is homework to do before we tackle our creative writing with serious intent.

The ability to focus is based on our ability to work on good ideas and inspirations. A good heading for a short story will almost write itself. An idea thrashed out will help it to germinate and guide your imagination in the right direction.

Let the ideas flow onto the page.

The following story is **focused** on a young tortured soul, unable to deal with her dilemma.

My Sea Friend

We met by chance, or did we?

I had a plan that centred on my being alone. No prying eye watching me, working out what I was up to. I'd had my fill of that. My life was my own business. How dare they pass judgement on me. Enough is enough!

There was a time when I relished someone caring, a chance to share. No. No going back. Get that thought out of my mind. I just wish those steely eyes would stop looking at me.

Should I wait? No. I've planned this time so carefully, nobody followed me. Nobody knows. How could they? How could anyone look into my mind and realize the anguish and sorrow that weighs me down. People. So thoughtless. Don't they realise a person wants to be alone. I'll just have to ignore them and wait.

Steely Eyes is still looking at me. Maybe we can have a telepathic chat. *'My name's Marie. What's yours?'* I'll call you Steve-with-the-steely-eyes, who spends time looking, but not touching. Oh, you don't like to touch? Imagine that.

I loved to be touched and caressed. But not anymore. He said I was too easy, provoked him. That's why he did what he did to me. Damaged goods. Who wants damaged goods with consequences? Well, Steely Eyes, have you something to say to me, telepathically? Silence. Just like my dad and my best friend who hate me. Oh, God, I can't bear it any longer.

Good. Those people are moving off. Too cold and windy by the sea, but not for me. It's a perfect day. I love when the sea is choppy, a perfect excuse for . . . I don't care if Steely Eyes keeps looking as I undress. I've given up caring about anything. No more tears or guilt. It will soon be over.

'Sorry? Did you say something?'

'Hey, miss, my family and I live around here. Tricky current. Wouldn't recommend swimming.'

'Oh, okay. Thank you.'

So, Steely Eyes, your fault I have to cancel my plan. Maybe I'm glad. Be my rock of strength if I come again. Maybe?

Create Pictures with Words

We are told that a picture paints a thousand words, helping us to realize the power of the visual. This is true and, yet, for the writer there is an art form to be gained by creating pictures with words.

Most people love to read, and so it is a wonderful gift to be able to use the right words to create pictures in the mind of the reader. We do this through our love for words.

This could well be a good place to consider how to write for Radio, where the listeners are dependent on words to create pictorial images.

As an exercise, write several examples beginning with a

COLOUR / SOUND / EMOTION

Instead of writing 'She walked into the room', use colour and emotion to create a picture i.e. 'The deep red velvet skirt made a swishing sound as she stumbled into the room, quietly sobbing.'

Here is an example of how to use this writing tool.

My Visitor

The doorbell rang. Strange, I wasn't expecting anybody. Who in their right mind would call around at 8 o'clock on a Sunday morning! Disgruntled by the disturbance, I rolled out of bed, wrapped my pink dressing-gown around me, and opened the hall door.

'My car . . . it just died,' the young man muttered, apologetically. 'Could I use your phone?'

Unimpressed by the youth of today, I stood back, pointing to the phone. As he stepped into the hallway, I became aware of how bad the weather conditions must be. His jacket, saturated by the rain, began to drip inconveniently on my polished floor.

'*Please,* your jacket. I'll put it in the hot-press while you make your call.' I was already regretting my good deed. Still, it would hardly be Christian to leave him at the door. Pity I was so quick to answer. Maybe he'd have gone to someone else, like the people down the road. No, they've gone away for the weekend.

Suddenly, it dawned on me how imprudent I was, opening my home to a stranger. Peter was constantly telling me, after I moved down to the country, 'Don't open your door to strangers. There are weird people going around these days.' I looked at the young man as he dialled his number and I felt no fear. He looked pathetic. He wasn't good-looking, just plain and thin, and definitely pathetic.

'Rain must be pretty heavy?' I dabbled at light conversation. He nodded in reply, as he spoke on the phone. 'Yea, I'm on my own. It's a cream-coloured bungalow, second turn left off the Dargle road, first house on the right.' He looked over at me. I relayed the name of my dream home, "Rainbow's End" with a little embarrassment. Peter had said it was a silly name.

'Nice name,' he said, as he passed on the information to his friend.

'I'll put the kettle on. Cup of tea, while you're waiting? Oh, you had better get out of that wet shirt and those pants too.'

He didn't say a word, just looked at me in a self-conscious way, then followed me into the kitchen. Skipping into the guest bedroom, I found a dressing-gown belonging to Peter, a bit on the large size, but warm. I struggled to hide a smile as I handed it to him. Maybe he was the one who wasn't safe.

While he changed out of his wet clothes in the bathroom and hung them in the hot press, I grilled sausages and pudding and brewed a pot of tea. The hot tea refreshed us both. I was now wide awake and curious.

'So, what's a fellow like yourself doing out on the road, so early?' He was embarrassed and muttered something about a party.

'Oh, I see. You were on your way home?'

He explained about his various friends who like to party at weekends. 'We sometimes keep at it 'til Sunday afternoon . . . you going to eat that last sausage?' I passed the plate to him and marvelled at his appetite. 'No food at the party?' I enquired.

'Yea, crisps and biscuits. And drink . . . is that piece of pudding up for grabs?'

After breakfast, I checked on his clothes: still damp.

'There's a bed in the spare room if you want to rest while you're waiting?'

He quickly took me up on the offer, and when I peeked in a half-hour later, he was fast asleep. His friend wouldn't be calling for at least two hours; plenty of time. I slipped out of the house without making any noise and enjoyed the walk to my local church in the village.

'Morning, Mandy. Nice fresh morning after all that rain. Where's that man of yours?' Fr Jack was always quick to get to the point. I nodded good morning and gave him my usual smile, as I passed on into the church. I like the Sunday service and meeting the local people, and the odd bits of gossip that seemed to be part of the Sunday ritual. Gradually, they had accepted me into the community. I ceased to be a stranger. When I joined the set-dancing classes, they welcomed me like one of their own. The past two years have flown by. I have lost any desire for city life and all that goes with it.

I was enjoying a cup of coffee in the local pub, arguing about the water rates, when I remembered my visitor. Better get back.

The front door was half-open. Close up, I could see the shadow of a man moving around. Filled with apprehension, I stepped into the hallway, armed myself with an umbrella, and with more bravado than sense, confronted the intruder.

'Peter, what are you doing here?'

He grinned from ear to ear as he replied, 'Wanted to surprise you. It's been over a week you know.'

I wasn't too happy to see him. 'Peter, we had an agreement."

'I know,' he cut in, but I missed you terribly. What do you say, we make a fresh start? Huh?' He took me in his arms and all my resistance began to fade away. Thinking back on it, my visitor's entrance at that moment was perfect timing. He sauntered into the room, bleary-eyed with Peter's dressing gown open at the front, revealing his underpants.

Peter was stunned into silence. His mouth gaped open, his brow furrowed, and his finger pointed at my visitor.

I simply looked at Peter with as guilty a look as I could muster. It has been over two years since I stepped away from my acting career, yet my performance proved to be of Emmy quality. Peter stormed out of the house, charged with rage at my 'infidelity'.

'Was that your husband?' asked my timid visitor.

I smiled. 'No, he's . . . he was a friend, of sorts. Fancy a cup of coffee before your lift comes?'

Goal Setting

A writer is one who writes, however, there are times when putting pen to paper does not come easily. There are various reasons for this.

Perhaps, this wonderful creative child hidden deep inside of us is afraid, just like a frightened child. Fear is a crippling weakness which all of us at some time or other will experience. The remedy is not always easy, yet to know there is a remedy is the beginning of being free from fear.

This is where **Goal Setting** comes in.

When we have a goal, perhaps a time-limit to come up with the next page of our book / story / article (whatever our creative work happens to be) then we can bypass our emotions, especially the emotion of fear. Work must be done, so we can and will put pen to paper.

Be deliberate. Set a goal that is realistic and must be fulfilled, and just see how the pen goes to work. Words will flow and a first draft will appear, encouraging you to write and keep writing.

REWARD: A word of encouragement

Sometimes, treating yourself by having a reward system can do wonders in helping you to write:

A special treat for two hours writing

A tasty meal for a whole day's writing

A special weekend for a good week of writing.

Try it and see if it works for you.

PART 3

The Art of Communication

It is vitally important in Creative Writing to be able to communicate exactly what you want to convey to your readers. Just as in life, we can spend time with people and come away with a different understanding of what they wanted us to hear. It can be commonplace for people to talk a lot without communicating.

Equally, we can use words that carry a different meaning from our readers understanding. Writers who wish to share their creative writing with others, know that quality and clear thinking must be invested in every written word. This is how good writing is created.

The death of a story or play happens when 'padding' is added to lengthen or emphasis what is taking place. It is a crime to bore our readers or audience with unnecessary words or dialogue. Become a wordsmith and make every word count.

The following piece shows how we can so easily manipulate the art of communication.

Tangled Web

It was a lie. I told myself it was okay. Yet that nagging, inner voice haunted me, chiding me.

A certain transparency takes place when you live with someone for twenty odd years. You become like one person with two personalities. I do love my husband.

I started seeing another man some months ago. How did I get into this mess? Should I tell him? I just can't. He would be wounded. I wouldn't, for the life of me, hurt him. Another lie.

I continue to tell more lies. I use my best friend Moira as my excuse. Paddy likes Moira. He often encourages us to go to the cinema, while he watches football matches on the T.V. I told my nagging conscience to shut up. I had every right to have a life of my own, didn't I?

Into my third month with Raymond, things got sticky at home. Paddy remembered my birthday (he never remembers my birthday) and decided to surprise me by taking me out for dinner and a musical show afterwards. Was I delighted? How could I be, it was the same night that I arranged to meet Raymond.

Becoming an expert at telling lies, I explained that Moira and I had already arranged to go out. Would he mind? Yes, he did mind. He confronted me there and then, wanting to know what was going on.

My only response was tears, plenty of tears, as I told him about Raymond and how I'd been meeting him every week for the past three months. Paddy was dumbfounded.

'He . . . he's an old man, for God sake!'

'I know, but he's a brilliant driving instructor and very patient with me.'

Using Our Imagination

Playing with words is always a good way to jump-start our imagination. Here are some examples:

Five-word challenge

Pick out 5 words at random and write them down. Write a story about an imaginary person using these five words. For example,

tractor, dog, fish, anxious, stone

Begin with a specific sentence

'I had no idea what would happen next . . .'

'It was beyond my wildest dreams . . .'

'It was a lie, yet I had no proof . . .'

Imagination needs some stimulation, so be adventurous. If you can think it up, it can become a reality to you and your readers.

Here is an imaginative, short dialogue piece:

Strange People

Grosinka stood motionless, out of view, behind the door. She had knocked, but there was no answer, so she stepped into the hallway. That is when she heard Mr Hardy's raised voice coming from the back kitchen.

'She's not moving in, do you hear me? And that's definite.'

'Is that so?' Mrs Hardy's voice cut through the air, followed by the crash of shattered glass.
Grosinka, afraid to move, remained hidden behind the door.

'My God, woman, what did you do that for? That's part of the crystal set we got for our wedding. Are you mad?'

'Yes, I am mad. Fit to burst. Now, either I get a yes from you or I'm going to smash every glass there is.'

Grosinka listened in disbelief. She regarded Mrs Hardy as a gentle, non-violent woman.

'Ah, Nuala, hold on. Can't we sit down and talk about this. You hardly know this woman, and you want her to live with us?'

'You big eejit Joseph Hardy, she's not going to live with us. She'll have the use of the caravan, out the back, and she'll help me with the housework.

'Still, Nuala, you don't know where these

people have come from. They're probably not even Christian.'

'And neither are we, Joe, if we turn our back on a homeless mother and child. My conscience won't allow that."

'Ah, you and your conscience. Remember what happened last summer when you took pity on those travellers. They robbed us blind, that's what they did.'

'We don't know for sure it was them.'

'Well, according to Garda Flannagan, it was a semi-professional break-in. Lucky enough we don't keep money in the shop overnight, but they broke the lock and stole 50 cartons of cigarettes.'

'If it were the travellers, they would have taken food too.'

'God above, Nuala, there's no sense in you at all. So that's what you want, you want us to be robbed blind again. Is that it?'

Grosinka struggled desperately to hold back a sneeze.

'She has an honest face.'

'Yea, heard that one before.'

Nuala moved closer to her husband. 'Have you forgotten, Joe, how it was for us, with the baby on the way and your family having nothing to do with us, and mine wanting me to give the baby away?'

'I remember.'

'If it hadn't been for that kind old couple, the Johnsons, giving us a place to stay . . .'

Joe became quiet for moment. 'I suppose you're right. Alright so. I'll give the caravan a quick clean-out.'

'Don't trouble yourself. You've enough to do with minding the shop. I've asked Grosinka to stop by and help me sort it out.'

'You said, yes, behind me back?'

'Sure, I knew you'd come around. Joe Hardy, you're a big softie with a loud bark.'

As they hugged each other, Grosinka wept silently moved by the kindness of Nuala Hardy. She tip-toed to the front door, gave a loud knock and waited. Maybe her people were wrong about the Irish. There are good people living in this wealthy country and she had found two.

A Question of Time

Have I **time** to write? A good question. Or more importantly, am I willing to give time to writing?

I love to write. When I sit down to write a story, or even a five-minute blog, I feel on top of the world. A deep hunger inside of me is being fed, and this makes me happy.

Perhaps my writing may prove to be of no commercial value, no matter, it does not take away from the proof that one is a writer and can write.

There are so many people who are interested in writing and yet fail to write.

REMEDY: **Time** is the remedy. Give time to writing. Time Management is the key.

This is the wonderful challenge in being a writer. Use a clock or a timer and plenty of goodwill.

Ask yourself: Am I a morning person and willing to rise early and write? Or perhaps a time that suits better is after breakfast, when you have a quiet space to write, and plenty of goodwill to do so. Being an evening person may prove more difficult, as it will infringe on your social life and time spent with others.

Again, it is back to goodwill and determination to follow all those wonderful inspirations that come to us each day.

Begin small with a weekly or daily creative thought. Or set up a BLOG that can be written in five or ten minutes. This can be so encouraging. Start with a word and inspiration will follow.

Because we are free from the pressure of having to come up with a story, or novel, or whatever, this exercise will inspire to write more and more.

Put it on our job list and it will become an enjoyable task.

Writing a Blog

For those who are not familiar with blogging, the method is quite simple.

There are many internet sites that talk you through the process of setting up a blog, but here are a few pointers:

1. **Pick a blog name.** Choose something descriptive e.g. Cáit's Creative Corner.

2. **Get your blog online.** Register your blog and get hosting. Word Press or Blogger are examples of software platforms.

3. **Start Writing**

Begin with a WORD. Even better, an inspiration. Fingers on the computer and, without thinking or dwelling on the word, just write what comes to mind.

We may at times surprise ourselves at what our subconscious mind releases. Do not allow that inner critic to peek out. Just follow the flow of what is coming to mind.

Five or ten minutes is a good amount of time for writing a BLOG. Of course, longer if we find ourselves with a strong flow of words.

Relax, take a moment, then read over what you have written. If you love it, post it, and maybe redraft it later if need be. If you do not like it, no worries, just scrap it and begin again.

Most important point to remember is that the very act of putting pen to paper and your fingers on the keyboard proves to yourself that you are a writer.

The following is my idea of a short **BLOG:**

DREAM ON

Someone once said, 'Poets and dreamers shake and shape the world'. Perhaps this can help us to put value on our dreams and aspirations.

Those of a spiritual mind believe we are inspired by God, much more than we might realize.
Do we listen?

Learn to listen well. This is the key to propel us forward and guide us in responding to our inner voice, prompting us to become more than we are.
If one is sincere about writing, then write!

The same will apply to a musician or artist and anyone who believes and is willing to respond to their creative mind.

What if . . .

When we look back on our lives, we see we have covered new ground. Perhaps there is something prodding us mentally about who and where we are in our lives. Are we who we want to be?

The invitation of this prompt is to look back and wonder, What if . . .

Was there a crossroads in our lives at one time? We made a choice and so we are where we are today, and, yet, What if . . .

We can go back as far as we want to - or feel inspired to.

Was it a job invitation?

Was it a friendship inviting us to take a certain road in life?

Family / Health / Faith? Take a moment to reflect and imagine ourselves as a different person.

The 'What if' prompt is a good exercise in character forming, and a great aid to creative writing.

Points to Ponder

Self-examination can help us realize that the characters we write about, especially in Creative Writing, might well be a part of ourselves.

It may be that our subconscious holds on to dreams, or even desires, that have filtered into our lives while growing up.

This gives us a wonderful opportunity to create *real* inspiring characters that propel our plays and stories forward, to capture the imagination of our readers, especially possible publishers!

Seems a shame to spend time writing good stories and plays and to just to leave them on the shelf.

Play the game of 'What If . . .' Surprise yourself with the strong characters that pop-off the page as you put pen to paper.

My 'What If' Story

When I was very young, living in Dublin, two friends and I went by bus to Sandymount instead of the regular sea-side trip to Dollymount, which was regarded as safe.

It was a huge adventure and we were filled with excitement and could hardly wait to put on our swimming togs and charge down to the sea. We decided to hold hands and support each other as we walked into the waves, laughing all the time.

What we did not know about was the under-current, and how quickly the tide comes in. Within minutes we were under the water without knowing what had happened.

Lucky for us, a man passing by realized we were in trouble. Then others came to help too. I felt a hand grab hold of me and pull me out of the water. I guess the same happened to my friends for, within minutes, we were all on safe ground again.

Between tears and laughter, we hugged each other, as our 'heroes' left us to it with strong advice, 'Learn how to swim before you do such foolishness'.

We made a pact never to tell our parents what had happened, and I made one with myself: learn how to swim!

Adversity

A special tool in writing creatively.

I love a good story with a happy ending. However, this could be boring for some readers, as one often likes a story with a 'bite' in it.

Perhaps, there is a bit of a devil in each one of us where we like to hear about something that shocks or unsettles us. That is why ADVERSITY is often necessary to prod us into action, and to come up with a good story line that our readers will enjoy.

It does not have to be gruesome, just perhaps bordering on 'edgy'.

The character we have chosen to be our hero can be betrayed in love / betrayed in friendship / vilified by lies of some sort or other.

It may break our hearts to have this happen. Yet the character must have opportunities to prove that they are, in fact, a real hero.

Adversity is often a good teacher of character strengths. If we dwell for a while on ourselves, we may be surprised, and perhaps encouraged, to see how our BAD days may often become our BEST days.

A troublesome day may well push us forward and extend our imagined limitations and often surprise us with abilities we did not know we possessed.

The same will take place for our hero. He or she will be forced to step up to the mark and let their good character be seen and admired.

How one deals with adversity is how one deals with life. So, let us be faithful to the characters we create, and let them be seen as real heroes.

The following story is about a young girl and a special friendship.

My Ray of Sunshine

He came into my life when I needed a friend. Not saying I have no friends. I have. They've been a real plus in my life yet, when the question of life and death entered my life, he became my special friend. I regard it as a real bonus, knowing him. His name is Ray.

I joke with him on my good days and call him my Ray of Sunshine. He smiles, holds my hand and I feel his special love for me.

I was preparing for college when it all started. It was meant to be a straight-forward medical check-up. I had received a scholarship through my excellence in sports, especially swimming.

However, the blood tests picked up a viral infection.

'A little set-back', Mum said. 'You're probably a bit run-down, what with exams and all that.'

Dad went out and got a special tonic drink. Said athletes drink it all the time to keep in shape. Dr Bates, our family doctor, put me on iron tablets. Uncle George had another remedy. So did Aunt Nora.

Yet, somehow, I knew. I didn't want to face the truth. I rebelled, went into denial, refused to go for more tests. Dr Bates stepped in and persuaded me to let the doctors in the hospital see what they could do. By now, my energy levels were pretty low. I found it hard to get out of bed. Everything became a huge effort.

Worst of all, was the fear gnawing inside of me, making it impossible to sleep. I was a wreck. Then Ray came into my life.

How did we meet? I can't fully remember. One day he was here in the hospital beside my bed. Perhaps he chanced into my room by accident, yet I don't believe it was by accident that we met.

My Ray of sunshine! When he was there, and Mum and Dad came in, I tried to introduce him, said his name. Must have fallen asleep. The painkillers do that. Make me so drowsy.

When I awoke, rays of sunshine shone through the window, lighting up the whole room, yet he was gone.

For a while, I didn't want other people to come and spoil our relationship, not even mum and dad. They were hurt, but all I wanted was Ray; to hear his sweet, comforting voice. Then, for some reason, he stopped coming. I was so miserable. Pain seemed to accelerate, and nothing could make me happy.

It was agreed to take me home. I guess the hospital gave up on me, but not mum and dad. I protested. I wanted to stay, hoping Ray would come back. Days past and I had to face the awful truth. He was no longer a part of my life. What good-looking fellow wants to spend his time with a miserable, sick girl. Or should I say, dying? Mum won't let me use that word. She believes in miracles. The only miracle I've known was meeting Ray, and now he's just a memory.

Though, it's not so bad at home. Mum and Dad have given me their bedroom with the big comfy double-bed that I used to snuggle into as a child. The en-suite is handy whenever the sickness gets really bad. I'm pretty tired most of the time, so the buzzer Dad has fixed up comes in handy. They say buzz anytime. I try to use it only for emergencies, which seem to happen more and more, especially when the pain killers wear off.

Mum has this fixation about rays of sunshine coming into the room, so she had the bed and furniture moved around so the rays would fall on me whenever the sun shines. I wish she hadn't, yet I say nothing. It hurts so much to think about

Ray. How could he abandon me like that? I try not to, but tears come, often.

Mum came up today. Said I would have a special visitor. She was so excited. Insisted on curling my hair and even dabbed a little rouge on my cheeks. I felt silly, a bit like a clown with my white face and ruby cheeks. I said nothing. I was kind of glad, for her sake. Lately, that has become a certain consolation for me, letting Mum and Dad do things for me. Most times, I have no interest, yet it seems to mean so much to them, and I enjoy seeing them smile again. Tears well up in my eyes, as I become aware of their tremendous love for me. Though I still miss Ray.

Mum wipes away my tears while dad props me up with pillows. They are so excited for me. Who could my visitor be?

They had barely left the room when he walked in. My Ray! I thought my heart would explode with happiness. He spoke in that lovely, soft voice of his, as he explained how he had to stay away for a while, for my sake.

Suddenly, I began to understand. Ray taught me how to love by visiting me and, somehow, he taught me how to share love by staying away. Yet all that mattered now was that he was with me. Ray offered me his hand and I gladly took hold of it. My joy was such that all my pain was gone, and I felt a wonderful peace of mind, body and spirit. I smiled, relaxing in his love, enfolded as if in a blaze of light.

From a distance, I watch as Mum and Dad step into the room, followed by Auntie Rose, my godmother. They stare at me and my smiling face, their eyes filled with tears, as they wonder at the lovely scent of perfume that emanates from the silent room.

PART 4

PLAYWRITING

What becomes most enjoyable about playwriting is being able to take part in someone else's life. For example, we start with an idea of someone who has a challenge in their life. Will it be something that will help them to develop as a person? Positive or negative, steps must be taken to lead this person into a way of dealing with their life for the better.

Tips for Writing a Play

In a play, the writing is set in dialogue. Still, there will be times when silence speaks louder than words: where less is more

Decide WHO is the main character. Allow the rest of the cast to support him/her, apart from the 'opposition' who will try to stop our hero from making progress. This will allow the plot to develop, bringing drama into the play. Be as true to life as possible, with room for comedy acts, as needed. Allow the characters to move forward, developing their style and voice.

Enjoy the process and the audience will enjoy it too.

THE FOOD OF LOVE

One-act Stage Play

By Vera Cáit Walsh

OUTLINE OF CHARACTERS

MRS MARY-ELLEN SWANEY: The widow

AGNES: Friend to Mary-Ellen - thin build.

DOLORES: Friend to Mary-Ellen - plump build.

DETECTIVE STACKET: Policeman

SALESMAN: Middle-aged opportunist.

LOCATION:

Sitting room in Mary-Ellen's home.

PERIOD:

Present times.

RUNNING TIME: 20 Minutes

SYNOPSIS:

Mary-Ellen believes the way to a man's heart is through his stomach.
Being a good cook, she is fortunate in her romantic life, yet not so fortunate in the demise of her several husbands! Like a well-made soup, the plot thickens as the 'LAW' steps in.

SCENE ONE

SITTING ROOM IN MRS MARY-ELLEN SWANEY'S HOUSE.

> MARY-ELLEN, in widow's drapes, comes into the sitting-room carrying a plate of cakes and walks over to her two friends, AGNES and DOLORES.
> Loud voices and clanging of cups and glasses can be heard in the adjacent room. DOLORES and AGNES sympathise with her, while they help themselves to her home-cooked scones.

DOLORES   Mary-Ellen, we are so sorry for your trouble. George was such a nice man, in his own way... Agnes, are all the chocolate eclairs gone?

AGNES   Indeed he was.
                 Sorry, Dolores, the crowd inside scoffed them.

MARY-ELLEN   George's family fancied
                    something sweet, after the
                    soup and the pot-roast. It was
                    so cold at the graveside

TEARS STREAM DOWN HER FACE.

DOLORES   There, there now. It was a
                    lovely funeral. They finished
                    off the pot-roast?

AGNES   Mary-Ellen, George, God rest
                    his soul, would have been
                    proud of you. Imagine
                    taking along home-made
                    liqueurs for your in-laws.

MARY-ELLEN   They're partial to a bit of
                    chocolate and I thought the
                    brandy would be appropriate.

DOLORES   They ate all the brandy-
                    liqueurs! Mary-Ellen, you're
                    too good.

AGNES   That's what I keep telling her.
                    Oh George, God rest his soul,
                    knew what a treasure he'd
                    found. Two blissful years you
                    gave him.

MARY-ELLEN   Almost three. We were
                    planning an anniversary
                    holiday for the month of July...

SHE BURSTS INTO TEARS.

AGNES	There, there now. Here's some tissues.
DOLORES one	I'll take the tray . . . goodie, butter-cake left.
AGNES	Mary-Ellen don't upset yourself. You've been such a good wife. Always slaving in the kitchen. Sure, you are practically a saint.
DOLORES	(With stuffed mouth) It's so true, it's the good people God puts to the test.
AGNES	Indeed He does. Mary-Ellen you've had more than your share of suffering . . . three husbands taken from you.
MARY-ELLEN	Yes. Three. First my darling Jimmy, and after he went, God rest his soul.
DOLORES	Came Paddy, the postman. Came quick and went quick.
AGNES	Yes, that was extraordinary, barely twelve months.

AGAIN, AN AVALANCHE OF TEARS FROM
MARY-ELLEN WHILE AGNES AND DOLORES
TRY TO PACIFY HER.
THEY ARE INTERRUPTED BY THE DOOR-
BELL RINGING.

AGNES	I'll get that. Sit down there Mary-Ellen and don't fret.
DOLORES	Don't worry Agnes, I'll mind her.

AGNES EXITS AND RETURNS, FOLLOWED
BY AN OFFICIAL-LOOKING MAN.

AGNES	Mary-Ellen, this is Detective Stacket, from the police.
MARY-ELLEN	Oh, I remember you. You were at the Inquest. Wasn't that strange, saying they didn't know the cause of death?
DETECTIVE	Mrs Swaney, could I have a few words with you.
DOLORES	What is it? She's just back from the graveside.
DETECTIVE	I'd like to talk to you about your husband, in private.
MARY-ELLEN	Yes, of course.
AGNES	Dolores and I will see how your in-laws are doing. . .
DOLORES	Do we have to?
AGNES	. . . and we'll be back shortly.

EXIT AGNES AND DOLORES

DETECTIVE STACKET PACES UP AND DOWN
FOR A MOMENT, THEN SITS DOWN
FACING MARY-ELLEN

DETECTIVE   Mrs Swaney.

MARY-ELLEN   Yes? You've something to tell
                   me about my husband?

DETECTIVE   Yes, Mrs Swaney.

MARY-ELLEN   He was a good man, my
                   George.

DETECTIVE   There's no question of him not
                   being a good man.

MARY-ELLEN   He just made the odd bet,
                   with the lads, on the
                   greyhounds. He used to keep
                   greyhounds, you know, in his
                   younger days.

DETECTIVE   Mrs Swaney, I have to tell you.

MARY-ELLEN   That accident, last year. It
                   wasn't his fault, you know, and
                   they took away his license,
                   wouldn't let him drive again.

DETECTIVE   Mrs Swaney.

MARY-ELLEN   Too old they said, and he
barely   a day over eighty. Those
                   heartless ones . . . they are
                   the ones who did him in.

DETECTIVE	What . . . what did you say, who did him in?
MARY-ELLEN	They did.
DETECTIVE	Who? Who are they? Mrs Swaney, you must tell me what you know.
MARY-ELLEN	It was them . . .
DETECTIVE	Who? I need names.
MARY-ELLEN	Sure, how would I know their names?
DETECTIVE	Well . . . have you any idea where I could locate them?
MARY-EL	The County buildings. That's where they hang out. Cheeky, heartless bureaucrats.

MARY-ELLEN SOBS NOISLY. AGNES AND
DOLORS COME RUNNING INTO THE ROOM

AGNES	Mary-Ellen, are you alright? You, what did you say to her?
DETECTIVE	I'm simply trying to find out who killed her husband.
DOLORES	My God, George was murdered?
DETECTIVE	We have reason to believe so.

AGNES	God rest his soul. Do you know who did it?
DETECTIVE	No, but Mrs Swaney does.

MARY-ELLEN CONTINUES SOBBING, OBLIVIOUS TO THE INCRIMINATION. AGNES AND DOLORES LOOK AT MARY-ELLEN, THEN LOOK AT THE DETECTIVE AND, IN UNISON, QUICKLY POINT TO THE FRONT-DOOR.

DOLORES	Please leave.
AGNES	Mrs Swaney is not available for questioning at present.
DETECTIVE	Very well, but I'll be back, tomorrow.

EXIT DETECTIVE STACKET

FADE TO BLACK

END OF SCENE ONE

SCENE TWO

THE FOLLOWING MORNING AS THE CLOCK
STRIKES TEN, MARY-ELLEN BLOWS HER
NOSE AS SHE STARES AT A PHOTO OF HER
DECEASED HUSBAND, GEORGE. EVERY-
SO-OFTEN SHE CHOKES ON A SOB.

MARY-ELLEN George, darling. Why did you
have to go and leave me
alone? You know I hate being
alone.

SHE SOBS TO HERSELF AND IS
INTERRUPTED BY THE OPENING OF THE
DOOR.

AGNES It's only me. How are you
today, pet?
Dolores is on her way around.

MARY-ELLEN Oh, Agnes, it's so lonely
without George.

AGNES I know dear, but you have to
be brave.

THE DOOR BANGS OPEN AND DOLORES
COMES RUSHING IN.

DOLORES You wouldn't believe it!

AGNES Believe what?

DOLORES Get over there to the window
and peek out.

BOTH AGNES AND MARY-ELLEN RUSH
OVER TO THE WINDOW AND STARE OUT.
DOLORES PULLS THEM BACK.

DOLORES   Discreetly. Don't let them see
                   you.

MARY-ELLEN   Who?

AGNES   Dolores, what are you talking
                   about?

DOLORES MANUEVERES THEM OVER TO
THE SIDE OF THE WINDOW AND
DISCREETLY PULLS THE CORNER OF THE
CURTAIN AND POINTS,

DOLORES   Now, do you see?

AGNES   My God!

MARY-ELLEN   I didn't see anything. What is
                   it?

AGNES   We're under surveillance. Do
                   you think they think we did it?

MARY-ELLEN   Who? Did what?

DOLORES   Maybe. We better be careful.
                   I've heard of people being
                   hanged without proof;
                   circumstantial evidence, they
                   call it.

MARY-ELLEN   Hanged? Whose being
                   hanged?

63

AGNES	Yes. We better be very careful. I wonder is it safe meeting here?
DOLORES	If we go somewhere else, they'll suspect we suspect.
MARY-ELLEN	Suspect what?
AGNES	You're right, Dolores. We'll just do what we always do, only careful like.
MARY-ELLEN	What's going on?
AGNES	Not a thing. Mary-Ellen, don't you worry yourself. Me and Dolores will take care of everything. Now, I'll go and put the kettle on. We are just three friends having a cuppa together.

EXIT AGNES INTO THE KITCHEN

DOLORES	Mary-Ellen, what's that lovely smell? You didn't bake . . . ?
MARY-ELLEN	Couldn't sleep, so I got up and baked a fruit cake.
DOLORES	We could have some with our tea? You rest yourself. I'll go and cut it up.

EXIT DOLORES INTO THE KITCHEN
MARY-ELLEN SITS BACK INTO HER SEAT AT
THE FIRE.
THE DOOR-BELL RINGS AND SHE MOVES
TO ANSWER IT.
AGNES AND DOLORES COME RUSHING IN
FROM THE KITCHEN.

AGNES   Don't. Don't answer it. We
        have to be prepared. Mary-
        Ellen, you sit back where
        you are. I'll go and bring in
        the tray.
        Dolores, you answer the door.

DOLORES   Why me?

AGNES GIVES HER A LOOK

DOLORES   Alright, but we have to watch
        what we say. Okay?

MARY-ELLEN SITS BACK, TOTALLY
CONFUSED. AGNES EXITS TO THE KITCHEN
AND RETURNS WITH THE FILLED TRAY.
DOOR-BELL RINGS AGAIN. DOLORES
EXITS TO OPEN THE DOOR.
DETECTIVE STACKET ENTERS.

DETECTIVE   Mrs Swaney . . . Ladies . . . do
        you live here?

AGNES AND DOLORES STARE AT EACH
OTHER.

MARY-ELLEN	Of course, I live here. This is my home.
DETECTIVE	I mean your friends.
AGNES	We visit, often.
DOLORES	Yes, we are visiting . . . now.

DETECTIVE STACKET LOOKS FROM ONE TO THE OTHER, TAKES OUT HIS NOTEBOOK AND WRITES IN IT. AGNES AND DOLORES LOOK FRIGHTENED.

MARY-ELLEN	Detective Stacket, it's nice of you to be concerned about what killed my husband. Did you know him? He never mentioned you . . .
DETECTIVE	Mrs Swaney.
MARY-ELLEN	. . . mind you, we did have separate friends, like me with Agnes and Dolores.
AGNES	Oh, but we knew George . . .
DOLORES	Yes, we liked him, God rest his soul, honest.
DETECTIVE	I see.

DETECTIVE STACKET AGAIN WRITES INTO HIS NOTEBOOK.
AGNES AND DOLORES BECOME MORE WORRIED.

MARY-ELLEN   I think I know what killed him.

DETECTIVE   You mean who?

MARY-ELLEN   My poor George, God rest his soul.

AGNES   (Whispers to Mary-Ellen) Careful what you say . . .

MARY-ELLEN   . . . it was the wind.

DOLORES   The wind killed George?

MARY-ELLEN   His stomach.

DETECTIVE   Mrs Swaney, what are you saying?

AGNES   Nothing. She's saying nothing. Can't you see the poor woman is demented after losing her husband. I think you should go.

DETECTIVE   And I think, it's time for Mrs Swaney to tell all she knows.

DOLORES   And what is it you think she knows?

DETECTIVE	The person, or persons who poisoned her husband.
MARY-ELLEN	Someone poisoned my George!!!

MARY-ELLEN CRASHES TO THE FLOOR IN A
DEAD FAINT. AGNES AND DOLORES RUSH
TO HER AID.
DETECTIVE STACKET MOVES NERVOUSLY
TOWARDS THE DOOR.

DETECTIVE	I . . . I must go, but I'll be back soon.

HE EXITS. **LIGHTS FADE.**

END OF SCENE TWO

SCENE THREE

AGNES IS PACING THE FLOOR IN MARY-
ELLEN'S HOUSE. MARY-ELLEN IS SITTING
IN AN ARMCHAIR BY THE FIRE, PLAYING
ABSENT-MINDEDLY WITH THE TONGS AND
HUMMING TO HERSELF. THE FRONT-DOOR
OPENS AND DOLORES COMES IN.

AGNES	Well?

DOLORES	They're still there, watching our every move. (Points to Mary-Ellen). Is she all right?
AGNES	Still watching us . . . oh, she's alright, I think.
DOLORES	Did she bake?
AGNES	Dolores, this is no time to be thinking of food.
DOLORES	It's not that. It's Mary-Ellen. She must be really bad if she's not cooking.
AGNES	I see what you mean.
DOLORES	Mind you, I wouldn't say no to a hot-buttered scone . . . Mary-Ellen, how are you pet?

MARY-ELLEN LOOKS UP FROM THE FIRE,
WHILE TEARS ROLL DOWN HER CHEEKS.

MARY-ELLEN	Dolores, this is a wicked world. Did you know they poisoned my George?

AN AVALANCHE OF TEARS FOLLOWS.
AGNES GOES TO HER AID WITH A BOX
OF TISSUES.

DOLORES	(To Agnes) What are we going to do?

AGNES	We are going to have no more nonsense, that's what.

AGNES BARGES OUT THE DOOR - HER LOUD ANGRY VOICE CAN BE HEARD IN THE DISTANCE.
SHE RE-ENTERS WITH DETECTIVE STACKET.

AGNES	We want you to explain to us what's going on.
DETECTIVE	Explain . . .?
DOLORES	Agnes . . . what . . . what's happening?
MARY-ELLEN	Oh, Detective Stacket, what a surprise. Please excuse me, I'm not well . . .
AGNES	We want to know what your game is. Why are we being stalked?

MARY-ELLEN AND DOLORES LOOK IN AMAZEMENT AT AGNES. DETECTIVE STACKET IS UNEASY.

DETECTIVE	Stalking . . . what are you talking about? I . . . we are just observing.
DOLORES	Observing whom?

AGNES	Us. That's whom!
DETECTIVE	Ladies . . . a man has been murdered.

MARY-ELLEN BECOMES DISTRAUGHT.

MARY-ELLEN	Someone else has been murdered? Oh, heavens preserve us . . .

AGNES AND DOLORES TRY TO PACIFY HER

AGNES	There, there, Mary-Ellen. Don't fret. Dolores and I are here.
DOLORES	Yes, love, we'll take care of you.

DETECTIVE STACKET TAKES OUT HIS
NOTEBOOK AND BEGINS TO WRITE

AGNES	What . . . what are you writing down? We're fed up with you, you know.
DETECTIVE	I have to do my job, no matter what. (To Agnes) Where were you on the night in question?
MARY-ELLEN	A night in question . . . is this a riddle?
AGNES	How dare you. For your information, I was with my friend, Dolores.

DOLORES	Yes, and I can confirm that.
DETECTIVE	I see. So you two were together on the night in question?
MARY-ELLEN	What's the riddle?
AGNES	Yes, we were. Satisfied?

DETECTIVE STACKET WRITES ALL INTO
HIS NOTEBOOK.
AGNES AND DOLORES ARE UNEASY.

DETECTIVE	Very well, then. I would ask, both of you not to leave town.
MARY-ELLEN	Girls, you never told me, were you planning on leaving town?
AGNES	Of course not!
DOLORES	Well . . .
AGNES	Well?
DOLORES	(Whispers to Agnes) The Antique sale. Don't you remember?
AGNES	(Whispers to Dolores) Oh, I forgot. Say nothing.

DETECTIVE STACKET COMES OVER TO
THEM, MENACINGLY.

DETECTIVE	Is there something you wish to tell me?
AGNES	No!
DOLORES	No, no. Nothing.
MARY-ELLEN	Oh, I remember. Girls, didn't you plan to go away, but George wouldn't let me come. Remember the big argument you had with him?

DOLORES STUFFS A PIECE OF FRUIT CAKE INTO MARY-ELLEN'S MOUTH.
AGNES HOVERS BETWEEN THEM, WHILE DETECTIVE STACKET WRITES INTO HIS NOTE BOOK.

DETECTIVE	Argument? With the deceased? Ladies, I advise you to come clean.
MARY-ELLEN	(With mouth full) Come clean? I'll have you know my friends are among the best dressed women in this community.
DOLORES	(Whimpering) It was only a little argument. He was bossy . .
MARY-ELLEN	Who was bossy?

73

AGNES	Yes, he was. He was trying to break up our friendship.
DETECTIVE	That's why you did it?
AGNES	We never meant him any harm . . .
DOLORES	We just didn't like the way he bossed Mary-Ellen around.
MARY-ELLEN	Who bossed me around?
DOLORES	George, God rest his soul.
MARY-ELLEN	My George? You're speaking like that about my George and he's not even cold in his grave.

MARY-ELLEN SOBS CONVULSIVELY.
DOLORES TRIES TO COMFORT HER, BUT
SHE PUSHES HER AWAY.
DETECTIVE STACKET WRITES IN HIS
NOTEBOOK.
AGNES COMES OVER TO MARY-ELLEN

AGNES	Oh, dear. Dolores didn't mean to upset you. We were just trying to stop George from bossing you around.
MARY-ELLEN	You too? And I thought you were my friends. Get away from me, do you hear!

AGNES AND DOLORES STAND AWAY FROM
HER, CRUSHED.
DETECTIVE STACKET PUTS A HAND ON
EACH OF THEIR SHOULDERS.

DETECTIVE   I must caution you . . .

DOLORES   (Whimpering) It was only an
                   argument.

PHONE RINGS. MARY-ELLEN PICKS IT UP

MARY-ELLEN   May I help you . . . Detective
                   Stacket? Yes.

SHE HANDS OVER THE PHONE TO
DETECTIVE STACKET.
HE TAKES THE PHONE, BARRING THE WAY
OUT AT THE SAME TIME.

DETECTIVE   What? But you said . . . I see
                   . . . very well.

HE PUTS DOWN THE PHONE. LOOKS AT
MARY-ELLEN, THEN LOOKS AT AGNES AND
DOLORES.

DETECTIVE   (To Mary-Ellen) On the night
                   your husband died, did he . . .
                   did you serve him a big meal?

MARY-ELLEN PROPS HERSELF UP WITH
PRIDE.

MARY-ELLEN   Indeed I did. We celebrated
                   him winning the Lotto.

DOLORES AND AGNES ARE ASTOUNDED.

AGNES

He won the Lotto?

DETECTIVE

So, that's why you did it.

MARY-ELLEN

Yes. He was so excited; wanted to take me out to a fancy restaurant.

DOLORES

Where did you go?

MARY-ELLEN

Didn't. Never know what you eat in those places. I cooked my special . . .

DOLORES

Not your special! Roast duck with walnut stuffing and oodles of gravy . . . mmmm.

DETECTIVE

That's what you cooked for your husband on the night of his death?

DOLORES

. . . and black gateaux delight for dessert?

MARY-ELLEN

I was thinking of it, but George, God rest his soul, was always partial to chocolate-chip pudding with double-cream chocolate dressing.

AGNES

I prefer your black gateaux delight.

DETECTIVE	Mrs Swaney, did you do it for the money?
MARY-ELLEN	Of course. We wanted to celebrate the winning. Sure it's not every day €100 is put into your lap.
DETECTIVE	€100! That's all?
AGNES	Not to be sneezed at. Mary-Ellen, did you spend it all?
MARY-ELLEN	Almost. We booked tickets for a Variety Show for the following night, but George took bad.

MARY-ELLEN SOBS NOISLY. AGNES AND DOLORES COMFORT HER.
DETECTIVE STACKET STANDS WATCHING, PUZZLED.

DETECTIVE	Mrs Swaney, did you know your husband had angina?
MARY-ELLEN	Oh, he got over all that stuff when we got married.
AGNES	George had angina?
DOLORES	What's angina?
DETECTIVE	How do you mean, he got over it?

MARY-ELLEN   Threw all that useless medicine
                    away. With me cooking good-
                    wholesome food, he was a
                    new man, God rest his soul.

AGNES   Can you just get rid of angina
                    like that?

DETECTIVE   So he never took his medicine?

        MARY-ELLEN, BRIMMING WITH PRIDE,
        LOOKED AT HIM.

MARY-ELLEN   Good, wholesome, home-
                    cooked food is the best cure
                    for all ailments.

        AGNES AND DOLORES STARE AT
        DETECTIVE STACKET'S TROUBLED FACE.

AGNES   (Whispers to him) All the rich
                    food?

DETECTIVE   'Fraid so.
                    The autopsy report states that
                    what was originally reported as
                    poisoning has turned out to be
                    a lack of medication. He was
                    congested with fat and his
                    respiratory system was . . .

MARY-ELLEN   My poor, poor George. I bet it
                    was those cigars. He
                    promised me he'd give them
                    up, but I know he used to
                    sneak down to the garden

shed and have one, on the sly.
Thought I didn't know...
I warned him. Said they'd be
the death of him . . . So, that's
what did him in?

AGNES AND DOLORES LOOK AT MARY-
ELLEN THEN LOOK AT DETECTIVE
STACKET.
HE LOOKS AT MARY-ELLEN, LOOKS AT
THEM.

DETECTIVE   Yes, Mrs. Swaney. That's what
                   did him in. God rest his soul.

HE CLOSES HIS NOTEBOOK AND IS
ABOUT TO LEAVE.

MARY-ELLEN   Oh Detective Stacket, I can't
                   let you go on an empty stomach
                   Sit down there and I'll cook you a
                   good wholesome meal.
                   Dolores and Agnes, you'll stay too?

DOLORES   I . . . I . . . Mary-Ellen, I . . .
                   I'm not hungry.

AGNES   Me neither. We . . . have to go.

DETECTIVE   Yes, me too.

DETECTIVE STACKET QUICKLY
MANOEUVRES HIS WAY TO THE DOOR
AND OPENS IT.
AGNES AND DOLORES RUSH AFTER HIM

SHOUTING THEIR GOODBYES TO MARY-
ELLEN.
MARY-ELLEN, BEWILDERED, STARES AFTER
THEM AS THE **DOOR SLAMS SHUT.**
MARY-ELLEN WALKS OVER TO THE FIRE-
PLACE. SHE FONDLES THE PICTURE OF
HER LATE HUSBAND, GEORGE.

A LOUD RING AT THE DOOR.
MARY-ELLEN TROTS OVER AND OPENS IT.
A SALESMAN PUSHES HIS WAY IN.

SALESMAN   Madame, a moment of your
                      time and I will show you how
                      to save a fortune with this
                      new carpet cleaner. A quick
                      demonstration?

MARY-ELLEN   That would be nice. It must be
                      difficult for you, going from
                      door-to door? I bet you're
                      hungry. Will I fix you a snack?

SALESMAN   Something to eat? Lady, you
                      know the way to a man's
                      heart.

MARY-ELLEN   Come on in. Sit down there by
                      the fire and I'll make us a
                      fresh pot of tea.
                      Help yourself to some of that
                      home-made fruitcake.

SALESMAN   Why . . . thank you kindly.

HE SITS DOWN BY THE FIRE, PLEASED AS
PUNCH. MARY-ELLEN HUMS TO HERSELF AS
SHE GOES INTO THE KITCHEN.

SALESMAN   (Munching on a piece of cake)
                  Ah, this is the life!
                  Not a bad-looking woman
                  either!

CURTAIN FALLS

P.S.

This play was performed in the Mermaid Theatre
as part of the Bray Drama Festival. We were one
actor short, so I was forced to make my debut on
stage as Dolores, the chubby, food-loving friend.
What a buzz!

WRITING FOR RADIO

Writing for radio is a great way to focus on dialogue, just as one would in writing a play. However, in a play we have visual images to offer our audience, whereas writing for radio is writing 'blind'.

The listeners to our radio play or story are dependent on what is said and, also, the use of sound effects. It can be great fun if correctly done.

There is also great freedom in writing for radio. The story can take place on MARS and with good sound effects and dialogue it can become a masterpiece. The writer could portray the West of Ireland simply by the way a person speaks in that part of the world. Without having to supply an image, the written word will construe the place and the people involved. It could also take place in London, or New York, or Japan. No need for elaborate sets or costumes.

Writing for radio can be demanding, as the story or script must be imaginative enough to entertain the listeners and hold their attention.

Also, leave room for the listener to use their own imagination and ability to see, without seeing, images happening in the story or play. This is the wonderful Secret of Radio.

Tips on Writing for Radio

Have a strong storyline and characters that compel people to listen and to enjoy listening. Present heroes that our listeners can love and villains they can hate, or at least feel sorry for.

Make allowance for a listener who may not have caught onto the characters at first, so a great help would be to repeat names and places frequently.
Add unexpected events and surprises, so the listening audience will want to listen well and be drawn into the drama.

Big challenge of radio is to entertain the listener.
Cut out all preaching about morals or such like.
Creative writing is a wonderful way to entertain and even move the listeners to tears or laughter.

Giving a talk on radio is something else. Practice reading out loud, so the timbre of our voice is relaxed. Radio is a great means of conveying and sharing our writings and ourselves with others, like a voice reaching out to the world.

Always enjoy what you write about, as if talking to a friend. The very tone of your voice tells a story.

Important: Write for yourself first. If good enough, share with others.

The following story for radio was prompted by a deadline.

Behind the Curtain

People say I'm nosey, maybe I am, yet it's amazing how much one can see from behind the curtain. And if it wasn't for me the other day, that little toddler would've got killed. Imagine, mothers out chatting, and the little chap crawled out onto the road. Lord, save us, you'd need eyes in the back of your head.

Awfully quiet now that the children have gone back to school and crèche and wherever else the mothers take them.

That meeting we had about a united community spirit never came to anything. Sure, almost nobody turned up.

Oh, a removal van, somebody moving? It couldn't be . . . not that new family. No sooner do you get to know people when they move out again. Course, the house is just rented, and such expensive rent from what I've heard. All this talk about Home Grants and a nice family like the Duggans can't afford to buy their own place. I wouldn't like to live in someone else's house. So important to have a home of your own.

Hmm . . . the two men have stepped out of the van. Quiet fellows. Hardly a sound opening the rear doors and releasing the lift thing at the back.

If only the binmen had the same respect for peace and quiet. The din they make would wake the dead. One of these days, I'm going to report them.

Now, isn't that nice. They've brought along dust covers and boxes. How thoughtful. Must write down their name . . . REMOVALS INC. No phone number. Pity, I like people who do a good job. Not like those fellows from the phone company spending hours putting in an extension in the bedroom and leaving bits of wire stuck into the carpet, and muddy boot-marks on the stairs. Their main interest was knowing when the kettle went on for a cuppa. In my day, people took pride in their work. Ah, these stressed-out times. All people can think about is money and time off.

That's strange. They didn't use a key to open the door. Maria must have left it open. Hard to remember with three little ones to look after. Must bake a cake, have the family over for a cuppa before they move off. I'll miss them, especially little Tommy. Took a fancy to me, so he did, calling me Granma. Maria says she hadn't the heart to tell him about his real grandma dying.

Ah, look at the way they're handling the furniture, as if it was their own. Oh, they're taking the TV as well. Oh, there's clothes in the wardrobe and that lovely red dress that Maria wore at Christmas. Oh, oh my goodness, they're not removal men - they're burglars! Oh, oh, he's seen me. He's telling the other fellow, sending him over here. Phone . . . must phone the police . . . 999. Help, help! What's the matter with this phone . . . no dial tone. Oh, oh, he's at the front-door, and he'll be able to get in without a key. Help! Somebody help me. Mustn't panic. Think, think! Oh, God, he has the door open. Under the stairs. . . hide there. Oh, my heart. Mustn't panic. Close over the door, quickly.

He's . . . he's moving around out there. Oh, God, hope he doesn't hear my heart thumping. Keeps calling me, says he won't hurt me. Mustn't make a sound. Can hardly breathe. He . . . he's opening the door. Aaahhhh, help me!

Ambulances are very noisy. I often wonder about that. Hospitals so quiet yet ambulances have that high-pitched screech. Maybe it's to make sure the patient is still alive. Oh, here comes the police officer. He looks awfully tired. Would you believe it, he doesn't like the sight of blood. A cup of tea will do us both good. Kettle's on the boil. Ah, that's better. I'm sorry about those fellows and look at the blood stains on the carpet. It'll take a bit of scrubbing to get them out.

Glad they're going to live. That wrench made a right gash on your man's forehead. Could have caused himself to be killed, frightening me like that. It's a good thing having the light meter under the stairs. Wonder is that other chap still shaking? Almost electrocuted himself, groping around in the dark. Must get onto the ESB about those old wires. Pretty silly of those fellows not to have torches. As I was saying, people just don't do a good job anymore, not even burglars!

Template

Enjoy the process of playwriting, writing strong characters to carry the story.

The following is the beginning of a play, *Lady Ivy's Demise*, set out for radio using an accepted template. For example, each speech should be numbered with each new page beginning with speech number 1.

There is no one correct way to format a radio play, but the golden rule is to follow the submission guidelines.

LADY IVY'S DEMISE

Radio play written by Vera Cáit Walsh

SYNOPSIS:
During the night, Lady Ivy's housekeeper, ELLIE, dies suddenly. The new doctor mistakes her for Lady Ivy and signs the Death Cert accordingly. However, for private reasons, Lady Ivy decides to play along as Ellie and so the drama begins.

MAIN SETTING:
Large drawing-room in a Grand Mansion with sounds of wind and rain.

CHARACTERS:

Lady of the Manor	Lady Ivy
Daughter-in-law	Mildred
Mildred's son	Phillip
Ellie	Lady Ivy's housekeeper
Derek	Ellie's 'nephew'
Estate Lawyer	Mr Gill
Young Lawyer	Mr Morris
Doctor	Dr Jones
Carer	Played by Ellie with different voice.

SOUND EFFECTS:
Creaky floorboards / dishes etc.
Garden sounds / birds / wind.
Sound of car, coming and going.

LADY IVY'S DEMISE

The drawing-room in a large Country Manor.
Lady Ivy is sitting at the table.
Her housekeeper **Ellie** comes in puffing.
She is carrying a laden tray.

1	<u>ELLIE</u>	Now ma'am, see what you think of this.
2	<u>LADY IVY</u>	Oh, Ellie, what a beautiful egg!
3	<u>ELLIE</u>	All the left-over porridge. Them hens love it.
4	<u>LADY IVY</u>	Why, it's nearly too good to eat.
5	<u>ELLIE</u>	Ma'am, you need to eat and build up your strength. You know well what Dr Brenner says.
6	<u>LADY IVY</u>	Oh, don't mind that old codger. Listening to him, you'd think I was made of china, ready to crack at any moment.

FX: She **cracks** the egg with a flourish

1 LADY IVY   What a beautiful yoke, and the toast is done to perfection.
Thank you, Ellie, you spoil me.

2 ELLIE   Ah, sure, somebody has to spoil you, with all the pressure from them good-for-nothings.

3 LADY IVY   Now, now, Ellie. They are family. I'm going to enjoy this lovely breakfast.
Why don't you join me?

4 ELLIE   I will not.
Maybe others have forgotten what a great lady you are, but not me.

5 LADY IVY   (Laughing) Great lady indeed. Oh, Ellie, you'd have me canonized tomorrow if you could.

6 ELLIE   And well you deserve some recognition for all you done for them ungrateful lot.

7 LADY IVY   Ellie, they are family.

90

1 <u>ELLIE</u>   If that's the case then I'm darn
                        glad all mine are dead and
                        gone.

Ellie leaves the room, **muttering** 'family
indeed'.
Lady Ivy **pours** herself a cup of tea.

2 <u>LADY IVY</u>   Dear Ellie, how she tries to
                        protect me. Perhaps there
                        won't be any calls today.

END OF SCENE ONE

SCENE TWO

Middle of the night
FX: SOUND OF MOANING.

Lady Ivy, startled, jumps out of bed and rushes
down the corridor.

3 <u>LADY IVY</u>   Oh, Ellie, what's happened?
                        Are you unwell?

Lady Ivy supports Ellie, who is **moaning in
pain**, back into her own bedroom.

1	ELLIE	(In pain) Ma'am, I can't . . .
2	LADY IVY	Hush, just lie down now. Be still. I'll phone Dr Brenner.
3	ELLIE	Ma'am, just one of me bad spells.
4	LADY IVY	We'll let the doctor tell us what's wrong. Sleep now, if you can, dear friend.
5	ELLIE	Oh, what a kind lady you are.

FX: She rushes to the phone dials the number

6	LADY IVY	(Whispering) Is Dr Brenner there? Oh . . . well is there another doctor? It's an emergency. Please come as soon as possible. Oh, to the Manor . . . Lady Ivy's . . . you know. Good.

With a deep sigh, Lady Ivy puts down the phone.

END OF SCENE TWO

SCENE THREE

Lady Ivy comes into the bedroom, followed by a young Dr Jones.

1 <u>LADY IVY</u>   (Crying) She . . . she doesn't seem well at all

2 <u>DR JONES</u>   I'll see what I can do.

He responds to Ellie's **groaning**, examining her.

3 <u>DR JONES</u>   This room is freezing. Please light the fire and bring more blankets.

4 <u>LADY IVY</u>   The fire? Blankets? Oh, yes.

She rushes out of the room
Ellie continues to **moan**
Lady Ivy returns immediately with blankets.

5 <u>LADY IVY</u>   I . . . must find some wood.

6 <u>DR JONES</u>   Never mind. She . . . she's gone.

Lady Ivy, bereft with grief, beings to sob.

<u>1 LADY IVY</u>	Oh, no. No!
<u>2 DR JONES</u>	You . . . you'd better take it easy. Put on some warm clothes.
<u>3 LADY IVY</u>	(Crying) She was my friend.
<u>4 DR JONES</u>	I'm sorry. It was pneumonia. I'll take care of the death cert.

He aims to go, pauses.

<u>5 DR JONES</u>	Will you be alright? Is there anyone else in the house?
<u>6 LADY IVY</u>	(Sobbing) Just the two of us.

Dr Jones opens his case

<u>7 DR JONES</u>	Here, take two of these with a hot drink. Will help you sleep. I'll call back in the morning. Okay?
<u>8 LADY IVY</u>	Dr Brenner?
<u>9 DR JONES</u>	Oh, he had a heart attack, but doing well. Don't worry, I'm available if you need me.

The doctor leaves the room.
Lady Ivy crumbles to the floor sobbing.

1 LADY IVY   Oh Ellie, dear Ellie.

END OF SCENE THREE

SCENE FOUR

NEXT DAY . . .
Lady Ivy, dozy from sleeping pills, comes
into the bedroom.

2 LADY IVY   (Shocked) What . . . what's
                    happened?

An older woman, a Carer, comes in

3 CARER   Oh, there you are. Been looking
                    for you.

4 LADY IVY   The . . . body?

5 CARER   Oh, undertakers were here.
                    Took care of everything.

The play continues . . .

POETRY

What is poetry? Poetry is a special form of written or spoken word, forming a pattern that puts emphasis on sound and the rhythm of words and their meaning. Poetry conveys a thought, an emotion, describes a scene, or tells a story in a lyrical arrangement of words, often using metaphor.

As a prose writer, more than a poet, I marvel at the skill of those who add such beauty and meaning into a line of poetry, such as William Shakespeare:

> *Shall I compare thee to a summer's day?*
> *Thou art more lovely and more temperate . . .*

Shakespeare's English is outdated and yet the sentiments are perfect in proclaiming love.

Another example of a love poem is found in Joseph Mary Plunkett's work. He was an idealist and one of the Irish Freedom fighters, almost a contradiction to the gentle and spiritual words of his poetry:

> *I see his blood upon the rose*
> *And in the stars the glory of his eyes . . .*

One of my favourite poets is Patrick Kavanagh, a countryman who wrote with such simplicity and beauty about the Irish countryside, where he grew up,

My father played the melodeon
My mother milked the cow

Nowadays, there is a drawing to Free Verse, and this is a wonderful practice for all writers. Free verse is a literary device that is poetry free from limitations of regular metre or rhythm and does not rhyme with fixed forms.

Whatever our 'writing voice' may be, as a playwright, screenwriter, or novelist, I would recommend reading poetry. Discover a poet that appeals to you and study the 'voice' of that poet, then begin, pen to paper, and write a poem.

Prompt:
Begin your poem with the words

'I looked, then looked away . . .'

It could well be you are a poet, yet do not know it!

Types of Poetry

There are many different forms of poetry, such as sonnet, limerick, ode, ballad and acrostic. Here are examples of a haiku, diamond and prose poem.

Haiku: a Japanese poem of seventeen syllables, in three lines of five, seven and five. Traditionally, the poem evokes images of the natural world.

> At risk of dying
> flowers wilting wanting rain
> refreshed with water.

Diamond Poem: makes the shape of diamond

> Alone
> I wait
> for morning light
> while shafts of colour
> shine brightly through my window
> I'll face another day
> respond with gladness
> good morning
> life!

Prose Poem: a piece of writing in prose having poetic qualities, including rhythms and imagery. This is an interesting way to play with words, poetically.

Here is one of my poems:

Dream On

Don't give up your dreams
just yet
let them smoulder like
an ebbing fire

don't let the flames
disappear
fan them to life
in a gentle way

don't let the effort
exhaust you
be ready, let the flames
explode.

The fire will rage
and dreams expand
fuel this fire
give it all you can

dreams come and go
almost like a whisper
fan the flame
let the inspiration flow.

The following poem expresses the restrictions we can put on ourselves when writing:

Ode to Freedom

Songbird imprisoned
      in the cage
what does it take
      to set you free
no outside lock imprisons now
for you yourself hold the key.

Here in the cage
you are well kept
with all that is needed
for life and health.

Yet no pampered care
can soothe your breast
for deep in your heart
there is no rest.

You hear a call
what can it be
but the call of the wild
to set you free.
Break the holding-chain
and try nature's gift to fly
beyond confinement bars and cage.

Raise yourself – reach for the sky.

Tom Walsh

SCRIPT WRITING

The format used in SCRIPT WRITING is essential if you want to interest publishers in reading your script. It could have started out as a novel, which has happened to many professional writers. Celia Ahearn's novel, 'P.S. I LOVE YOU' is now a well-known movie.

It is an advantage to be able to redraft your own work, a novel, or whatever it might be, and have the wonderful opportunity to see your work put up on the 'big screen'.

If the task becomes difficult, we can avail of a Script Writer to format our creative writing for us. However, it is wonderful to be able to script write yourself. 'We are the Captain of our Ship . . .'

The following **Love Song** is a short story scripted for television.

LOVE SONG

BRIEF SYNOPSIS:

The screenplay LOVE SONG is about an ordinary girl, Mary Collins who is faced with a difficult challenge, a willingness to break away from past fears and take a chance with life and love.

CHARACTERS:

MARY COLLINS	Single, thirties
JACK	Former friend
ELLIE	Mary's roommate
SOLDIER	USA soldier based in Dublin
Extras	Waiter in restaurant and couple.

SETTINGS:

DUBLIN APARTMENT

RESTAURANT

CANAL BANK near Patrick Kavanagh's bench.

1.
Fade in

INT. DUBLIN APARTMENT
LATE AFTERNOON

MARY COLLINS comes into frame, followed by her roommate, ELLIE.

>ELLIE
>Mary, please, he's a really
>nice fellow.

Mary turns around and faces Ellie.

>MARY
>Why can't we make it a foursome?

>ELLIE
>I... I said that to Eddie, but they don't
>really get on well together. You know
>what brothers are like.

>MARY
>He can't get on with his brother,
>and you want me to go out with him!

Ellie comes over to Mary, leans forward, confidentially

>ELLIE
>I think Eddie is going to propose

>MARY
>Tonight?

ELLIE
Yes! I'm almost sure.
The other day when we were
in town, he got me to try on
some souvenir rings.
Oh, Mary, I'm so excited.

MARY
Ellie, I'm so glad for you.
For sure, this is what you want?

ELLIE
Yes. Eddie's the one for me.

Mary is quiet for a moment, then pulls
herself together.

MARY
Okay, I'll do the noble deed,
and babysit his kid brother.

ELLIE
Mary, you're a real pal.
Enjoy yourself. A night on the
town; a free meal; who knows,
maybe we'll be planning a double
wedding. Imagine that.

Mary throws a book at her.

MARY
Ellie, you are such a romantic.
And you don't have to butter me
up anymore. I said I'd go.

Mary begins to put on her coat. Ellie stops her.

> ELLIE
> Oh, I said you'd wear pink.

> MARY
> Pink!

> ELLIE (cont.)
> . . . so he can identify you.

Mary shrugs her shoulders, resignedly.

> MARY
> And how am I supposed to identify him?

> ELLIE
> He'll wear his American uniform

> MARY
> Oh great, a show-off.
> What's his name?

> ELLIE
> Bud.

> MARY
> Bud! You're joking?

Ellie sheepishly shrugs her shoulders.

2.   **INT. RESTAURANT   EVENING**

MARY, wearing a pink blouse, sits nervously at a small side table in a not-so-busy restaurant. She watches as a young couple come in and the waiter brings them to a centre table. They look happy.
Mary's thoughts drift away.

3.   ***FLASH BACK***

CUT TO: DIFFERENT RESTAURANT
SIX MONTHS PREVIOUS

Mary walks up to a table and is greeted by JACK LYONS

> JACK
> Mary, I was getting worried.

Mary sits down

> MARY
> I went for a long walk.
> I, I had to . . . think.

Jack is apprehensive.

> JACK
> And?

> MARY
> I'm sorry, Jack.

JACK
May I ask, why?

Mary is close to tears.

MARY
Because I don't love you, and I
don't think you love me either.

JACK
I've asked you to marry me.

Mary places her hand on his

MARY
Jack, you are a dear friend.

He pulls his hand away.

JACK
Friend? We've been seeing
each other for almost a year.

MARY
I know. We . . . I like being with
you, but it wouldn't be right to
marry, without love.
Oh, Jack, I've seen it with many
of my friends. It doesn't work.

Jack looks at Mary, a pained expression on
his face. Then he gets up and quickly walks
out.

4. **CUT BACK TO** **PRESENT-DAY**
RESTAURANT:

With a deep sigh, Mary opens her eyes and
looks up at a tall uniformed soldier
hovering over her.

> SOLDIER
> Hi, bet you're Mary,
> Ellie's roommate?

Mary stares into his rugged, tanned face
and at his deep, beautiful eyes

> MARY
> Yes, I am.

He remains standing.

> SOLDIER
> Ellie said you'd be wearing pink,
> but forgot to say, look out for
> the finest-looking gal in the
> room.

> MARY (flattered)
> You probably say that to all
> the girls.

> SOLDIER (smiling)
> Only the good-looking ones.

He looks at her for a moment. She smiles.
He sits down.

> SOLDIER
> Would you like a drink?

                    MARY
            Sherry, please, sweet.

He calls over to the waiter.

                   SOLDIER
            Waiter, could we have a beer,
            and a sherry . . . sweet.

He looks at Mary when he says SWEET. She
blushes. He then takes out a pack of
cigarettes, offers her one.

                   SOLDIER
            Smoke?

                    MARY
            No, and neither will you.

She points to a NO-SMOKING sign
He grins and puts away the cigarettes.

                   SOLDIER
            I ought to give them up, anyway.

He smiles. Mary smiles. A moment of
silence.

                   SOLDIER
            Say, would you fancy a meal?

                    MARY
            That would be nice.

They wine, dine, chat and laugh together.
Mary studies him, now and then, without
being noticed and likes what she sees.

                      109

5.   **EXT. RESTAURANT EVENING**

They come out of the restaurant, still
chatting.

> SOLDIER
> Gee, thanks for a great evening.
> Will I get you a cab?

> MARY
> No thanks, I'd prefer to walk.

> SOLDIER
> Good. I'll . . . walk you home.

> MARY (smiling)
> This way.

6. **EXT. GRAND CANAL   MOON-LIT EVENING**

They walk along the Grand Canal, chatting.
When they come to the sculpture of Patrick
Kavanagh, they stop and sit each side of
the seated figure.
Mary puts her hand on the sculptured
shoulder.

> MARY
> This is my favourite poet

> SOLDIER (reciting)
> 'She looked as if she didn't see.
> He looked as if he didn't care,
> Yet I heard by telepathy
> the story of a love as rare
> as ever trembled in the air . . . '

110

Mary is amazed.

> MARY
> Why, that's my favourite
> poem, Patrick Kavanagh's
> Love Song.

> SOLDIER
> We get quite a bit of leisure time
> so I like to study, and read poetry.
> Aiming at doing a course in English
> Literature, here in Dublin.

He becomes a little self-conscious.
Mary looks at him with new-found
admiration.
They continue their walk, discussing poets
and poems and lyrics and singers.

7. **EXT APARTMENT BUILDING   NIGHTTIME**

> They arrive at the front door of apartment
> building.

> MARY
> I, I'd invite you in, only . . .

> SOLDIER
> I understand.

He looks at her for a moment, then bends
forward and kisses her.
Mary responds willingly. They remain
kissing, then he looks at her
and slowly walks away.
Mary looks after him.

                    MARY
            Bud . . .

He turns around and looks at her.

                    SOLDIER
            Oh, Bud couldn't make it.
            Say, do you think he would
            mind. I mean . . . if I were to
            ask you out?

Mary beams with happiness.

                    MARY
            No, **I** wouldn't mind.
            By the way, what's your name?

        ENDS.

            FADE OUT

(10 min. script)

MEMOIR WRITING

Writing a memoir is not the same as writing an autobiography - it is just one or more stories from your life.

Discovering who you are requires certain questions to be answered, before you begin your journey. I have outlined some questions you can ask yourself, objectively. This brings us back to our roots and choices we have made in life:

Who   Who am I?
Why   Why am I the person I am?
Where   Where did I begin?
When   When did I decide about my life?
How   How did I become me?

Writing exercise

Re-invent yourself as someone else. This is also a good template for writing characters.

The following is a memoir I would like to share with you about my childhood.

Childhood Colours

My parents had a grocery shop at the top of Capel street, near Bolton Street College, in Dublin. This was our home. It was the fifties, a time of innocent poverty with no frills, yet I felt rich and happy. My memories of childhood, playing games on the street are linked with pastel colours and grey skies, like a Monet painting.

My summer holidays were spent with my grandparents in their cottage in the hills of Donegal. My pastels changed to vibrant colours, sky-blue, corn-gold, like the bright paintings of Van Gogh. Summertime involved haymaking and trips to the bog to collect the turf. Occasionally, a car trip was arranged to Bundoran with its beautiful, long golden beach, trimmed with blue-green sea and decorated with shimmering, white waves. My uncle called them white horses. To me they represented images of angels playing hide-and-seek in the sparkling sea.

Some days were grey when it rained. Yet even then, there was the mystery of shaded lights as the tilly lamp was lit and the cottage-kitchen became a library where books and comics, and even coloured catalogues, were avidly read. The inner light of reflection was fostered and appreciated.

Returning to Dublin filled me with mixed emotions of happiness and sadness. I trembled with excitement as the taxi pulled up outside our shop, newly painted in vibrant red. Our name, WALSH, shone above the door, dazzling in the sunlight, as if a Divine Hand had turned on a giant spotlight. Daddy came out to greet us, his smiling face charged our hearts. I ran to hug him and vied with my siblings for a chance to be lifted up into the air in his arms. As he helped the taxi-man with the bags, I studied this wonderful man and my heart flooded with love at the sight of him. All without words, yet volumes were spoken in our hearts.

In the days that followed, we resumed our regular routine. Mammy would call me for 7.30am Mass in St. Saviours Church, Dominick Street. The dark, winter mornings presented a challenge, yet afforded me a chance to have Mammy all to myself. On the way to Mass, I could talk to her about anything and everything. Coming home was spent in respectful silence, and our shared silence created a special bond.

Arriving home, I removed the bolts from the shop door and took in the morning papers from the hallway, while Mammy prepared breakfast. Daddy removed his bike from the hallway and set out for work on one of the new building sites in Dublin.

The shop became busy as people dropped in for their morning papers and cigarettes and groceries. We were used to having our meals interrupted. Mammy would often take her cup of tea with her as she served the customers and chatted with them. Her kind nature was far too soft for a person of business, yet I've no doubt she was rewarded ten times over for her acts of kindness and generosity to those in need. During the day, cups of tea and even bowls of soup when available, found their way into the newspaper corner where Mammy spend time listening and encouraging those who sought her out. Her wisdom came from her prayer-life, mingled with natural common-sense.

School was often a challenge. My world of soft pastels turned to grey as I worried about the ability to learn. Mammy would listen and help sort out the difficulties of my muddled mind. However, when it came to complaints, she admonished us, 'Teachers have a tough job, so don't cause any trouble. Learn your lessons and be good'. Mammy understood the challenges of teaching a class of 56 pupils.

I remember one teacher who would often rant and rave. We learned not to listen. She left.

Her replacement was a young nun. This made us nervous. You don't misbehave with nuns and get away with it. What a happy surprise to find a smiling face. She was interested in teaching us.

Her methods were different. It was as if she played games with us, and taught us simple ways to remember our grammar, and stuff like that. Most of all, she taught me that learning can be painless. It can even be fun!

At ten, I began to realise that adults are like grown-up versions of children They need plenty of colour in their world too.

NOVEL WRITING

It is possible that everyone who wants to write will discover a novel hidden deep within their creative self. If we have a good idea of ourselves and our taste, then we will be drawn to the kind of novel we would like to write.

Next step is **passion**, a deep and wonderful passion for what we want to write about. Will it be romantic, philosophical or drama? Whatever we can be passionate about will guide us.

Having a strong desire to write is a huge plus, because then we will have no trouble in applying ourselves to the discipline of writing.

 Now that we have ourselves roughly sorted, the next step is **Time.**
Seasoned writers tell us that time is of the essence when it comes to writing.
Passion will drive us to spend hours applying ourselves to our writing. Next day, the bubble may well have burst, and we have difficulty in applying Pen to Paper.

Therefore, a chosen time to write each day is of huge benefit and avoids us becoming a victim to emotions and moods. Remember: a writer writes!

Novel Writing Guidelines

It is important to be passionate about your writing. Here are the main points to remember:

THEME	Subject
PLOT	Action
VIEWPOINT	Whose story is it?
PLANNING	Don't rely on memory, keep notes
CHARACTERS	Work out their history, name, age, family, taste
LENGTH:	Good average is 80,000 words
CHAPTERS	30 of 2,500 words roughly
METHOD	Basic Chapter Guideline:

1	Beginning
10	Special moments
15	Conflict
20	Change of events
25	Puzzle solving
30	Resolution.

Characters

Show genuine interest in the characters. This way you help the reader to be interested in and care for them too.

Dialogue

How we speak is an indication of who we are.
Same applies to each character we create.
Study how dialogue is set out in modern novels.

Plot

Plot develops through conflict.
Become involved with the people and their story.
Allow drama to unfold.
Highlight all that is positive and all that is negative.
Find balance in the novel, just as in real life.

Style

Our style defines who we are, so be true to oneself.
Originality is precious. Do not 'copy-cat'!

The following is the beginning of a novel based on
a young girl called Mimi.

Mimi's Story

Mimi was usually quiet and friendly, but not today. One of the other girls in the Home Shelter had mentioned about the injections. Mimi was terrified of needles.

'Oh, bother,' complained Nora, the resident nurse. 'Everything was going so orderly and this had to happen.'

'We found her hidden away under the bed,' replied Charlie, the maintenance man, as he held on to Mimi with a firm grip. Mimi screamed and begged to be left alone, but Nora coaxed her with a cup of hot chocolate.

Eventually, Mimi calmed down as she sipped her drink, unaware that Nora had mixed in a strong sedative. By that time the bus, with the rest of the girls, had departed. They would have to bring Mimi by car. Such a nuisance. Charlie carried a drowsy Mimi down to the car and placed her in the back seat.

'We'll have to miss lunch,' said Nora. She checked that Mimi was asleep, then tucked her in with a warm, woolly rug. 'I wasn't prepared for this,' Nora grumbled, as she squeezed into the passenger seat and put on her seatbelt.

'Don't worry,' Charlie reassured her as he quickly picked up speed on the motorway. 'I know a nice Deli, just off the highway.'

'They ought to send out a doctor, instead of us having to cart everybody off to the Clinic,' Nora moaned.

After a while, Charlie pulled into a garage. Nora pointed over to the Deli.

'Listen, I'm popping into the 'ladies' first. You keep an eye on Mimi.'

Charlie nodded. He peeked in and smiled at the sleeping bundle. Mimi was in dreamland.

Mimi was floating on a bed of clouds, happily bouncing up and down while distant voices and noises hummed a chanting, relaxing sound. All was well. She was safe and had no need to worry. Then, suddenly, a white-coated person with no face came towards her, waving a gigantic needle. Terrified, she began to whimper and sob.

Mimi woke up with a start. It was only a bad dream, she sighed. Or was it?

WRITING FOR CHILDREN

Writing for children is quite an achievement. There are so many requirements to be considered, and yet, it is such an enjoyable ability to develop. The gift of helping a child to be creative, imaginative, and interested in writing is rewarding in itself.

Children live in the moment and need stimulation to read and be moved by what they read about. Illustrations or pictures can be of great benefit.

Most children have a natural interest in nature and animals. The hero of a story could well be a dog or a cat, and this is accepted as a reality in the mind of a child.

Judging by the number of fantasy books, there is a great need for heroes. If a young boy or girl is willing to step up and become a hero and help to save the world, then that would make a good story.

The world of fantasy is especially interesting. The idea of having special powers and abilities to invent ways of making the planet a better place has a natural appeal. We have great examples of a world of fantasy and magic in the Harry Potter stories. Also, there are wonderful stories of families who travel around the world and introduce us to places we might never know about. Some stories take us into the future and how it will be 100 years from now.

An imaginative story about space travel and the earth 200 years from now, could be a good challenge for a writer and, taking into account the reading ability of an older child, this could well be a winner.

The following short story is suited for 6 to 7-year-olds.

Christmas Story

It was Christmas eve and there was sadness in the Tracy family. First of all, their father's flight had been delayed, coming from London. Then Noel heard his mother talking on the phone. She was on the verge of tears.

'But you must come. How else will we receive the Christmas presents?'

Noel quietly tiptoed into his sister's bedroom and woke her up. Sally did not like to be woken up. She questioned Noel about the bad news.

'How do you know it was Santa that mummy was talking to?'

Noel paced up and down the room, feeling more and more sad.

'Who else could it be? Who else brings the Christmas presents except Santa?'

'Do you think he found out about what we did. About playing tricks on cranky Mr Granby?' asked Sally.

Noel suddenly stopped pacing up and down. 'Of course. That's it! Santa knows everything, so he would know. But Mr Granby is an old crank, always giving out to us when we play in the garden or slide on the ice. He doesn't even like to hear us laughing.'

'It's not fair,' said Sally, feeling gloomy, 'but the truth is we were mean. Mummy says we should never be mean, even when people are mean to us. We ought to have goodwill at Christmas time, for everybody, even the people who don't like us.'

Noel began to think, 'I know what we can do so Santa will come with our presents.'

Sally jumped up and down on the bed with excitement. 'What . . . what can we do?'

Noel became serious, then he spoke. 'We must go around to Mr Granby and tell him we are sorry for ringing his doorbell and making him angry all the time.'

Sally looked at her toys and play-stuff. 'I'll give him a present of . . . Sam.' She lifted up her precious little teddy bear and hugged it.

'And I'll give him my . . . my best comic book,' said Noel.

Decision was made. Sally quickly dressed herself and she and Noel decided to sneak out of the house. Of course, they were not allowed to go out after tea, but this was special and had to be done.

They were as quiet as mice as they climbed over the garden wall into Mr Granby's garden, but when they tried to get through the side entrance to his house, the gate was locked. There was nothing for it but to knock at the backdoor.

They had to knock several times before the door opened. Mr Granby stood there, an angry look on his face. 'What's going on here?' he asked impatiently, as he shivered in the cold night air. 'What do you want?'

Sally was too frightened to say a word. She simply held out her precious teddy bear and thrust it into Mr Granby's unwelcoming hands. Noel handed him the Iron Man comic that he treasured. 'These are for you for Christmas,' he said.

However, words failed Noel when it came to saying sorry for knocking at Mr Granby's hall door during the week, so he just stood there in silence.

Mr Granby glared at them in disbelief.

'What? I, I can't take your gifts,' he stammered.

Sally began to cry. 'Oh, please, if you don't, Santa won't be able to bring us our presents.'

Noel joined in, pleading with Mr Granby. 'Please, sir. Please accept our presents for you, for Christmas.'

Mr Granby hesitated for a moment, then quietly accepted the gifts that Sally and Noel presented to him. Was that a smile on his face? Noel looked closely at him. Because they had never seen Mr Granby smile before, they could not be sure. They noticed the wet look in his eyes. This probably meant that he had a cold. Maybe that's why he was so grumpy all the time.

These were the thoughts Noel and Sally shared as they managed to climb over the garden wall and back into the safety and warmth of their own home.

Later, in the middle of the night, Noel woke up. The phone was ringing. Mrs Tracy rushed to answer it.

'Oh, thank God. So, you will make it? And you have all the presents. Oh, Noel and Sally will be so happy. I love you.'

Noel smiled to himself. So, Santa would be coming after all. Yet, he wondered what his dad would think of his mum telling Santa that she loved him!

PART 5

Finding Your Voice

If we ask ourselves what genre we most enjoy writing, then we have a good idea of our 'writing voice'. There are so many diverse ways of being creative with words, so it is good to explore and give time to writing and discover our true selves.

Playwriting came to the forefront for me, often from short stories I had written, which I felt needed to be voiced. It is wonderful to see a piece of creative fiction come to life on a stage. Maybe, for me, the next step will be the 'big' screen! One can always dream.

Study

They say, learn from the best, so read or go on YouTube, and study writers who have proved their writing skill.

Find out about writers that you admire and how they managed to make a success of their writings. Find your voice and your writing will flow effortlessly, like a gentle stream.

I believe I found my writing voice when I began to write about my childhood memories and stories that I had read and wanted to believe in.

When I found myself inspired to write about these events, which meant a lot to me as a child, I suddenly realised that I had discovered my 'inner' self which led to my creative voice. The way I write and put sentences together reveals to me a pattern of my writing skills.

Such a gift to find one's voice!

Search Party

When we feel at sea about our writing abilities, then we can go on a Search Party to find ourselves. Our creative child can easily get lost in a world of extensive reading and writing. Begin with the local library and scan through several books, beginning with those that appeal to you.

Next, spend some time scanning through books that do not at first appeal to you. Remember, we are on a search for our writing voice, therefore, all this time given to research is of value. You will surprise yourself by your discoveries.

A Healthy Mind

Health experts tell us that a good night's sleep is essential for a healthy mind, and the same applies to being a good writer.

Of course, we hear stories of people who stay up all night and write. If they can do so, fair dues, yet a person who is sincere about writing, and perhaps working on their first novel or play, needs to be sharp and alert to the inspirations that come.

Keep in the flow. Make it a pleasant and enjoyable experience to discover and follow new inspirations. The beauty of writing is found when we love to write. And, just like life, our efforts will demand time and a quiet space so we can listen to the wonderful thoughts coming our way.

At one time, I was a total novice in relation to writing, yet found myself eager and hungry to write creatively. I told myself I would do it for fun and write just for myself. When I decided to submit a story to a magazine, I was surprised to find it was accepted and published. What a pleasant way to earn a living.

My final story, *The Petticoat Train*, was prompted by a trip to my grannie's home in Donegal, many years ago. Now a piece of social history.

The Petticoat Train

The excitement was almost unbearable as we charged along Amien Street station, my mother in front carrying the baby. Mr Peel, my father's friend, was struggling with a large suitcase, while my older brother, Liam, followed close behind with the medium case. The rest of us followed suit. Mairead, my older sister, pulled Michael, the second youngest, after her. He was crying, said he had to pee. Thomas, my senior by one-and-a-half years, held my hand and practically dragged me along. I held on tightly to my holy-communion bag, which contained my new shiny rosary beads and my pocket-money.

Mr Peel shouted back to us, 'Keep up, keep up or you'll miss the train.' He didn't have to shout, after all, it was all his fault for putting us on the Belfast Express. Pity Daddy had to stay home and mind the shop. He wouldn't have mixed up the trains. Only that Mammy asked, we would have been on our way to Belfast. The other passengers lifted us off the train, throwing the good suitcases after us, just before the train pulled out.

Then the panic began to find the right train to take us to granny's. People stared, some amused, at our unusual procession as we scurried past them.

'Donegal Express? Better hurry, it's ready to pull out,' said the ticket-man, adding to Mammy's nervous state, and our general confusion. How could the train go without us? Didn't they know we weren't on board yet?

'For God's sake, hurry,' cried Mr Peel, his face purple from the exertion of carrying the big suitcase. Liam was silent, yet his red face and deep breathing spoke for the weight of his suitcase. Michael continued to cry as Mairead half-carried him along. Thomas took my hand and began to pull. I wanted to stop and rest. My breathing felt funny, my head too.

In the distance, the stationmaster stood ready with a whistle in his mouth. He caught sight of us and gestured for us to hurry. By now, I could hardly breathe. Thomas held tightly to my hand and wouldn't let go, pulling me after him. The stationmaster ran down to us, opened a door and, with the assistance of the passengers, we were all hauled on board. The whistle blew and we were on our way. As the train sped out of the station, we waved goodbye to Mr Peel. He managed a short wave as he stood slightly bent over, becoming smaller and smaller.

As soon as the train left the station, Mammy and Mairead took the younger ones to the toilet. Liam and Thomas went exploring while I sat there, recovering. It was so nice, just to sit and be quiet and watch the countryside whizz by the window.

'Our Father, who art in heaven . . .' I looked around and realised all the people in the carriage were reciting the rosary. I was used to the family rosary at home, but all these people praying together made me feel shy. Timidly, I took out my brand-new holy communion rosary-beads and whispered my response. I noticed a few smiles on the faces of the people nearby. I felt good and proud of my new rosary-beads. Then I remembered what Sr Eilish had said about pride and tried to be unproud. Mammy and Mairead returned and joined in. Then I wasn't shy or proud anymore, just comfortable, like at home.

Sometime later, after the rosary was finished and Mammy had got chatting with the other women, and everybody admired baby Vincent, I went exploring with Thomas. He didn't want me coming with him, but I insisted. 'This is my train too,' I replied to all his protests about girls not being explorers. He gave in and grudgingly let me follow him. However, when we came to the joining part between the carriages, I hesitated. The walls squeezed in and out, and the floor kept moving.

'Told you, girls are no good at exploring,' said Thomas, as he ran ahead, reaching the safety of the other carriage. I was terrified yet had no choice. I had to pretend not to be afraid. I nervously put one foot forward, then another, then froze. Surely the train was going to break in two and I'd be thrown onto the tracks and killed dead.

'Here, let me help you.' A tall man in black lifted me off my feet and placed me on solid footing. I looked up at him, 'Thank you, Father.' Thomas jeered me about having to get help from a priest. Did I think I was going to die? If he only knew the truth, but I would never confess.

The next carriage was packed solid with grown-ups. No children at all. The women admired my new dress and pretty ribbon, asking us where we were going.

'To our granny's,' replied Thomas.

'And where might that be?' asked one of the women. 'In Petticoat,' I said, proud to have remembered the name. 'Our Uncles James and Thomas-Sean will meet us there and take us to Granny's cottage. It's got real straw on the roof, and a half-door, and the chickens fly in over it.'

The women laughed. Had I said something funny? Then one real nice woman produced a bar of chocolate and gave us half each. A whole half-bar of chocolate each! One of the men came over and gave us each a new shiny penny, saying we might like to light a candle when we go to church.

'Do we have to?' I asked as I followed Thomas back through the 'divider'. This time, I held on to the back of his jacket, then I wasn't afraid.

'He only said *might like to*,' said Thomas as he added the penny to his pocket money. I put mine into my holy-communion bag. I could ask Mammy if I should light a penny candle. Anyhow, we didn't often get to Church, sometimes not even on Sunday if the horse wasn't well. Then, Uncle James and Thomas-Sean would go on their bikes and we would listen to Mass on the radio with Granny.

When we found our way back to our place on the train, Mammy was handing out sandwiches. We came back just in time before Liam scoffed most of them. Then we each got a whole small bottle of lemonade. Mammy said to eat quietly as most of the passengers were fasting. They mustn't have had anyone to make sandwiches for them. One of the women nearby gave Mammy a cup of tea, out of a flask. It was piping hot. Mammy was so pleased.

Baby Vincent was sound asleep in Mairead's lap, so Mammy and the other woman had a great chat about growing up in Donegal, and the dancing on a Saturday night and the fun they had. Each home would take it in turns to have the neighbours in. The furniture would be pushed back, and the flagged floor left free for dancing. I listened with great interest to stories Mammy had never yet shared with us, and said, no, to a second exploring trip, even when Thomas invited me to come.

I must have fallen asleep. Mammy was shaking me. 'Come Cáit, put your coat on and get your bag. We're coming into the station.'

'Are we in Petticoat?' I cried out with delight. The men and women nearby began to laugh, assuring me that, yes, we were at last in PETTIGO.

'Enjoy the holiday at home with your mother,' said the tea-woman to Mammy, as we parted company. 'God speed to you on your pilgrimage to Lough Derg,' said Mammy as the woman and her companions made their way toward the buses.

'Do all those people go on a praying holiday?' I asked Mammy making our way to the tea shop where Uncle James would be waiting.

'You could be right there, Cáit,' said Mammy. 'A pilgrimage to Lough Derg is a spiritual holiday where a lot of prayers will be said.' I looked back at the large group of people who had already begun to say another rosary. I thought, 'Maybe when I'm bigger, I don't know.'

However, at that moment, all I could think of was the hot-buttered scones in the tea shop and meeting Uncle James, and the horse and cart trip out to my granny's cottage in the hills of Donegal.

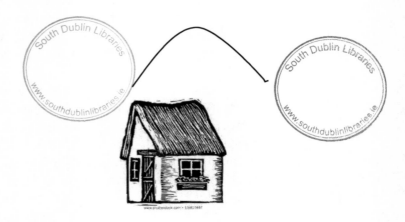

136

Conclusion

My main reason for writing *Pen to Paper* is to encourage others to write while, at the same time, introducing the positive side of Creative Writing.

I have always had an interest and love of words, and when the idea of writing a book came to mind, I realized it would be a wonderful way to share my love for this creative art. I hope that has come across in the many examples of different forms of writing, using the prompts and exercises throughout the book for inspiration. I especially hope that you have enjoyed my stories, memoirs, plays and poems.

Writing is meant to be a fun practice where we can facilitate our creativity, and even learn more about ourselves through the inspirations and ideas that come to mind.

Now, put pen to paper and let's write!